EMS Law

A Guide for EMS Professionals

Richard A. Lazar
Attorney at Law
Portland, Oregon

AN ASPEN PUBLICATION®
Aspen Publishers, Inc.
Rockville, Maryland
Royal Tunbridge Wells
1989

Library of Congress Cataloging-in-Publication Data

Lazar, Richard A.
EMS and the law: a guide for EMS professionals/ Richard A. Lazar.
p. cm.
"An Aspen publication."
Includes bibliographies and index.
ISBN: 0-8342-0042-2
1. Emergency medical services--Law and legislation--United States. I. Title.
[DNLM: 1. Emergency Medical Services--United States--legislation. WX 33 AA1 L4e]
KF3826.E5L39   1989   344.73'03218--dc19 [347.3043218]
DNLM/DLC
for Library of Congress
88-39436
CIP

"This publication is designed to provide accurate and authoratative information in regard
to the Subject Matter covered. It is sold with the understanding that the publisher is not
engaged in rendering legal, accounting, or other professional service. If legal advice or
other expert assistance is required, the services of a competant professional person should
be sought." From a Declaration of Principles jointly adopted by a Committee of the
American Bar Association and a Committee of Publishers and Associations.

Editorial Services: Mary Beth Roesser

Library of Congress Catalog Card Number: 88-39436
ISBN: 0-8342-0042-2

Printed in the United States of America

1 2 3 4 5

To Michelle, for her love, support, and red pen, and to Cace the dog, for keeping my feet warm during the long hours in front of the keyboard.

Table of Contents

About the Author

Preface

During the past several years, I have lectured emergency medical technicians (EMTs), paramedics, and emergency medical services (EMS) administrators throughout the United States about EMS and the law. I also have participated in EMS litigation in several parts of the country. These experiences have reinforced my view that politics is *the* most destructive force in EMS today.

I have identified many problems inherent in EMS systems throughout the United States. Many of these problems relate to system designs and the effects of politics on these designs. Having been influenced by politics, many prehospital care systems pose real dangers to patients in terms of quality of care.

It is inevitable that EMS systems molded by political rather than quality-of-care influences will injure patients unnecessarily. These patients then will sue justifiably prehospital care providers to recover damages resulting from their injuries.

My hope is that the information provided in this book will result in changes in prehospital care delivery systems. If EMS administrators recognize the liability potential of a given system component, that component will be fashioned with the patients, rather than the system participants, in mind. Such recognition, I believe, will result in better-designed EMS systems and higher quality patient care.

The overall goal of this book is to improve prehospital care through an educational process because educated EMS professionals are less likely to make mistakes. To be effective, the lessons learned throughout this book must be translated into changes in prehospital care systems. However, EMS systems can be designed to minimize litigation potential only if EMS leaders set aside politics and turf battles and keep patient interests foremost in mind.

I thank all participants of my EMS LAW seminars throughout the country. The stories you shared aided in the development of many field incident examples used throughout this book. Your candor and enthusiasm are very much appreciated.

Table of Cases

Chapter 1

Introduction

1.1 INTRODUCTION

The legal system represents a complicated set of abstract principles. The emergency medical services (EMS) system personifies a
complicated blend of people and events. The interrelationship
between these two systems is at the heart of this book.

Many members of the prehospital care community fear litigation.
This fear is based in large part on a lack of understanding about the
law and its operation. This book is designed to educate prehospital
care providers about the legal system. It is hoped that education will
allay fears of the unknown.

Although this book offers EMS providers information about the
legal system as it applies to prehospital emergency medical care,
questions about the legal system will arise nonetheless. The law
provides no clear answers to legal questions faced by EMS professionals. Instead, the law presents only imprecise guidelines that help
predict what an outcome *may* be. After reading this book, an emergency medical technician (EMT) will possess the tools necessary to
evaluate a prehospital care incident and to assess the potential liability of the people involved.

Many examples are used throughout the text to articulate the legal principles being discussed. Because of the complicated and changing nature of the law, the alteration of one significant fact within these examples could change the entire legal analysis and outcome. This also is true in real life: An EMT who performs one way in a given case may be found to have acted responsibly; however, a slight change in the course of the EMT's conduct in a similar case may result in liability.

Study of this book does not guarantee that an EMS provider will never be sued. However, through education, the number of lawsuits against EMTs, paramedics, and other prehospital care providers can be reduced. EMS professionals who follow the principles discussed throughout this book will be in a better position to defend against a lawsuit should litigation occur.

It is true that in the field of law, as in many other fields, the best defense is a good offense. Knowledge of laws that apply to prehospital care is one way to avoid litigation. However, the best and most important way for EMS professionals to avoid lawsuits is to use common sense when treating patients.

1.2 LIABILITY POTENTIAL OF PREHOSPITAL CARE PROVIDERS

Statistical information and liability research on EMS is scarce and difficult to obtain partly because, historically, a central clearinghouse or library for EMS information was never established. However, more data on the assessment of the liability potential of prehospital care providers is being made available. For example, in one liability study conducted in 1985, the liability potential of prehospital care providers was examined.[1] Specifically, in that study, the malpractice actions against prehospital care providers in a large advanced life support urban EMS agency were examined over a ten-year period. The agency studied was the Metropolitan Dade County (Florida) Fire Department, which serviced, during the period of the study, an approximately 2,100-square-mile area of greater Miami and a population of approximately 1.7 million people.

Between 1972 and 1982, the fire department responded to 265,000 incidents, using twenty-eight advanced life support (ALS) ambulances staffed by three paramedics each. During those years, sixteen claims were filed against the Dade County EMS system. Six claims involved response time problems; four, mechanical equipment failure or patient-lifting injuries; and six, allegations of professional negligence.

Results of the study showed the ratio of claims to the number of rescue incidents as one claim to 24,096 responses. The average annual incidence of claims in the Dade County EMS system was 1.03 claims per 100 paramedics. During the 10-year study, approximately one out of every 100 paramedics in Dade County could expect to be sued annually.

Can the information derived from the Dade County system be applied to every urban EMS system? Probably not. The liability potential of EMTs and paramedics varies depending on the communities served and the number of calls run.

Although little data on the liability potential of prehospital care providers exist, the data that do exist suggest that the likelihood of being sued is minimal. If the results of the Dade County study reflect national expectations, only slightly more than one out of every 100 paramedics who work in an urban EMS system will generate a claim annually. Careful and conscientious EMTs may never be sued; however, if sued, such EMTs will be in a much better position to defend the lawsuit.

1.3 SUMMARY OF CHAPTERS

The chapters in this book build on each other in many respects. For example, later chapters presume an understanding of earlier chapters. Chapter 2 focuses on the legal system and its components. "The Law" is defined and an overview of the anatomy of a civil lawsuit is presented.

Chapter 3 explores in detail the concept of negligence. The elements of negligence are discussed and negligence principles are applied to specific prehospital care incidents. Defenses to negligence actions also are presented.

Chapter 4 focuses on the standard of care, a subcomponent of negligence. In Chapter 4, the standard of care is defined and readers will learn how to comply with it to avoid liability.

Chapter 5 examines the complicated issues of consent and refusal. The concept of legal capacity, including a discussion of the treatment of minors, is explored first. Then, the issue of mental capacity, including discussions about competence and the means and scope of consent, is presented.

Chapter 6 addresses the issue of abandonment. Discussions about the EMT–patient relationship and termination of this relationship are presented.

Chapter 7 examines the concept of vicarious liability. The notion of indirect legal responsibility for EMT conduct is examined, particularly in the employer–employee context.

Chapter 8 involves records and record keeping. The purpose of medical records as well as right-of-access to medical records is discussed. Also, the use of medical records in litigation is explored.

Chapter 9 examines the important concept of quality assurance. Components of a quality assurance program are presented in the context of quality assurance program goals.

Chapter 10 addresses questions about insurance. A discussion of the types and purposes of insurance is presented.

Finally, Chapter 11 focuses on governmental responsibilities in connection with EMS system design and operation. Potential legal ramifications of various governmental choices in the prehospital care setting are explored.

1.4 CONCLUSIONS

Overall, this book is designed to provide prehospital care providers with the tools to avoid litigation. The information in this book must be learned and used carefully before any benefits can be enjoyed. If but one negligently induced patient injury is prevented and, therefore, one lawsuit is avoided, this book will have served its purpose.

NOTE

1. J.M. Soler, "The Ten-Year Malpractice Experience of a Large Urban EMS System," *Annals of Emergency Medicine* 14 (October 1985):87.

Chapter 2

The Legal System: An Overview

2.1 THE LEGAL SYSTEM

To understand the duties and responsibilities required of prehospital care providers, it is important for the emergency medical technician (EMT) to gain a basic understanding of the legal system. The legal system represents a complex mix of law and procedures designed to evaluate and process claims of one individual or entity against another. This chapter presents the EMT with an overview of the law, including an examination of where "the Law" comes from. A summary of the steps involved in a civil lawsuit also is explored. Throughout this chapter, the discussion of the legal system focuses on *civil* law, which differs from *criminal* law.

The purpose of criminal law is to prevent harm to society. Criminal laws declare what conduct is unacceptable to society and prescribe the punishment to be imposed for such conduct. The broad aim of criminal law is to prevent injury to the health and safety of the public. This aim is accomplished when the government prosecutes individuals on behalf of society. Prosecutors seek to protect societal rather than individual interests.

Lawyers, such as local district attorneys, who represent "the state" in a criminal case must prove beyond a "reasonable doubt" that the

5

person charged with a criminal offense has violated some criminal statute. To establish this difficult standard, a prosecutor must convince a jury, to a moral certainty, of the guilt of the person accused of the crime. The punishment for conviction can be imprisonment, a fine, or both.

In contrast, the purpose of civil law is to enforce, redress, or protect private rights. All law that is not criminal in nature is civil. Using the civil law, individuals and organizations seek to correct or recompense private wrongs. Negligence, for example, is a private wrong. When a person is injured because of another person's negligence, the injured person seeks compensation through the civil law. The injured person seeks civil redress against the wrongdoer to protect the private right not to be injured by the other person's negligence.

The injured person in a civil lawsuit must prove by a "preponderance of the evidence" that the injuries received resulted from the negligence of another. *Preponderance of the evidence* means greater weight of the evidence or more likely than not. This standard is less demanding than the "beyond a reasonable doubt" standard of the criminal law.

EMTs should note that a negligence lawsuit brought against an EMT does not mean that the EMT is a poor technician. Instead, a person who brings a negligence lawsuit is saying that the EMT made a mistake in that instance for which compensation is allowed. EMTs sometimes have difficulty keeping this idea in focus in the context of an ongoing lawsuit. Only the conduct of the EMT in the specific circumstances that result in the lawsuit is examined—not the EMT's conduct in general.

In the United States, unlike some countries, violations of private rights generally do not result in criminal prosecutions. Thus, an EMT found negligent will not be required to pay a criminal fine or go to jail. Thus, the focus of this chapter and this book is on the civil law.

2.2 CIVIL LAW: AN OVERVIEW

"The Law" is a body of rules derived from various sources that have a binding legal effect. The law must be obeyed and followed by everyone. Violations of the law subject the violator to sanctions or legal consequences. The rules that make up the law provide guidelines within which society functions. Everyone is affected by the law every day—almost every aspect of our lives is governed, in some fashion, by

rules of law. Rules of law primarily come from two sources of law:
(1) written law in the form of legislation and (2) decisions by courts of
law.

All levels of government have the power to enact laws. At the federal
level, Congress enacts laws in the form of statutes that affect many
different types of conduct, including EMS conduct. A statute is
an act of Congress that declares, commands, or prohibits something.
Congress may delegate enforcement of statutes to administrative
agencies or states. Administrative agencies then may enact rules
implementing the statutes. For example, Congress enacted a law
requiring ambulances to meet certain construction and safety standards. The General Services Administration then adopted specifica-
tions that set forth the specific design and construction standards.[1]

At the state level, state legislatures pass laws in the same manner as
Congress. State legislatures also can appoint state agencies to regulate state law. For example, in Oregon the State legislature enacted a
law requiring that EMTs be certified.[2] The legislature appointed the
State Health Division to adopt rules specifying exact certification
requirements, including educational requirements.[3]

At the local level, municipalities pass laws in the form of codes or
ordinances, which also may affect emergency medical services (EMS).
Nationwide, such codes and ordinances are not as common as state
or federal laws that govern EMS. For example, a municipal ordinance
may set forth the local standing orders or protocols.

Generally, each state has the power to enact laws governing the
health, safety, and welfare of its citizens. Occasionally, federal laws
may conflict with state laws. The courts then may be called upon to
determine the law that has priority. However, the statute generally
takes precedence when a state statute and a local ordinance conflict.
Therefore, if local protocols conflict with state mandates, the state
prevails.

In addition to settling state–federal law conflicts, courts also interpret and apply written laws, such as statutes and administrative
rules, to particular cases. Courts determine the rights of individuals
based on preexisting standards set by previous court determinations. Courts interpret laws and, in doing so, may create law. Court
created law is known as *common law*. Courts also decide whether a
legislature or administrative agency is acting within the scope of its
authority. Agencies are bound by the statute that empowers them.
Agencies also are restricted by federal and state constitutions. An

agency acting outside the scope of its statute or the state constitution can be restricted by the court.

Individual cases are determined by trial courts; however, the rulings may be appealed to appellate courts. These higher appellate courts rely on *judicial precedents* to determine the outcome in a particular case before them. Judicial precedents are derived from written legal opinions that set forth legal standards developed in similar cases decided earlier. These opinions create the common law comprising the vast majority of the law books found in any law library.

The following case example is the first of several to be used throughout this book. Each case includes a *legal citation*. Legal citations are a means of identifying and locating a court's written opinion. A particular case can be found at a local law library, which usually is located in the county courthouse or local law school. Within the library are law "reporters" that contain all of the written opinions from courts around the United States. Table 2-1 includes the reporters and their abbreviations.

A legal citation consists of three component parts: (1) a volume number; (2) a reporter name (by abbreviation); and (3) a page number. For example, 450 So.2d 881 means page 881 of volume 450 of the second series of the Southern Reporter. To find this case, simply locate the reporter series identified by the abbreviation, find the volume number shown before the reporter abbreviation, and turn to the page number following the reporter abbreviation. Citations to

Table 2-1 Legal Reporters

Reporter	Abbreviation
Atlantic 2nd	A.2d
Pacific 2nd	P.2d
North Eastern 2nd	N.E.2d
South Eastern 2nd	S.E.2d
North Western 2nd	N.W.2d
South Western 2nd	S.W.2d
Southern 2nd	So.2d
New York 2nd	NYS2d
Federal Reporter 2nd (Fed Circuit Ct)	F2d
Federal Supplement (Fed District Ct)	Fed Supp
U.S. Supreme Court Reporter	U.S.

state reporter volumes precede the citations to the reporters listed in Table 2-1. Ask the law librarian for assistance.

Case Summary 2-1

Case Citation. Franklin Ambulance Service v. Dept. of Health and Rehabilitative Services, 450 So.2d 580 (Fla. App. 1st Dist. 1984).

Facts. An ambulance service's license to operate was revoked by the Florida Department of Health and Rehabilitative Services on the grounds that the service violated numerous statutory and administrative rules. The health department contended that the ambulance service failed to maintain continuous phone access by the public, failed to have certified EMTs attending patients, and kept false records. The ambulance service then appealed the administrative agency's decision to revoke its license to the Florida Court of Appeals.

Court Ruling. The court allowed the administrative agency's decision to stand, thus affirming the license revocation.

Analysis. The state of Florida's legislature passed statutes and promulgated administrative rules setting forth ambulance service licensing requirements. The Department of Health and Rehabilitative Services, the agency responsible for enforcing these laws, sought to revoke an ambulance service's license on grounds that the service violated the state's licensing requirements. The court was called upon to determine whether the administrative agency was correct in taking revocation action.

The ambulance service was affected by numerous law sources. The statutes and administrative rules set forth the requirements that an ambulance service must meet to obtain and keep an ambulance service license. These statutes and administrative rules required constant phone access, EMT patient attendance, and accurate record keeping. Once the administrative agency suspected violations of these laws, the ambulance service had the right to adjudicate its rights in an administrative hearing.

After the hearing and the decision by the administrative agency to revoke the license, the ambulance service sought court intervention. The court was asked to interpret the statute and its rules and to allow the ambulance service to keep its license. The court gave deference to the agency and accepted the agency's interpretation of the rules. The court further upheld the agency's findings that the ambulance service violated the law and its rules. Thus, the agency's decision to revoke the license was allowed to stand.

Exercise. List all of the sources of law that affected the ambulance service in the *Franklin* case.

The law, from all of its sources, affects every aspect of prehospital care. EMTs must be aware of all statutes and administrative rules affecting the profession. Being aware of the sources of law and the contents of law represents the first step in complying with the law. Knowing the law is the best way to avoid violating the law.

2.3 ANATOMY OF A CIVIL LAWSUIT

When an EMT negligently injures someone, the injured person uses the civil law and the civil courts to seek compensation for the injuries. This section examines why and how a person sues an EMT, what the EMT can expect after the lawsuit is brought against him or her, and how the legal system processes negligence claims. Although negligence is not the only type of lawsuit that can be brought against an EMT, it certainly is the most common. Therefore, this section focuses on the steps of a civil negligence lawsuit.

2.3.1 Suspicious Incident

A *suspicious incident* is an incident that involves injury and may result in a lawsuit. The incident is considered suspicious because injury is evidently caused by wrongdoing; however, no one has sued anyone yet. Consider the following example.

Field Incident Example 2-1

Facts. An ambulance responds to the scene of an automobile accident. The driver of one car complains of numbness in the legs coupled with neck pain. Upon arrival at the hospital, it is discovered that the driver is a quadriplegic.

The EMT did not immobilize the patient's neck before removing him from the car. Only after the patient was placed on the stretcher and the stretcher placed in the ambulance was a short spine board and cervical collar used. This set of facts alone does not disclose any negligence. However, the patient believes the EMT, not the accident, caused his quadriplegia. Based on this suspicion of substandard care, the patient contacts a lawyer. The patient's lawyer believes the EMT was negligent and that this negligence resulted in the severe spine injury.

2.3.2 Case Investigation

Before any lawsuit is brought, the lawyer hired by the injured driver conducts a case investigation. This investigation is designed to determine whether, in the lawyer's opinion, the EMT improperly treated the neck injury and whether the improper treatment, if any, caused the quadriplegia.

The attorney utilizes a number of sources of information to investigate the claim. State laws, administrative rules, and standing orders are examined to see if the EMT and the EMT's employer complied with them. These laws help the lawyer determine whether the ambulance was properly staffed and supplied. The lawyer obtains and examines in detail the prehospital care report form completed by the EMT for standard of care compliance. Textbooks, journal articles, and local protocols are consulted to determine the proper way to treat suspected neck injuries and to assess whether accepted procedures were followed. Witnesses to the treatment are interviewed for their perceptions of what happened at the scene before transport.

Finally, a medical expert is consulted to evaluate the EMT's conduct. The expert usually is a physician who specializes in emergency medicine and has experience in prehospital care. The medical expert renders an opinion whether the EMT acted negligently in treating the automobile accident victim.

2.3.3 Filing the Lawsuit

Because the lawyer believes the patient's claim has merit, a *complaint* is prepared. A complaint is a document outlining the negligent conduct of the EMT. Exhibit 2-1 is a simplified sample complaint for Field Incident Example 2-1.

The patient's lawyer then *files* the complaint with the court; that is, the complaint is presented to the court, which assigns the case a court number. This is the formal beginning of the lawsuit.

The *parties* to the lawsuit, those individuals or entities directly involved in the lawsuit, are listed always at the beginning of the complaint and all subsequent court documents. The *plaintiff* is the person bringing the suit—the person claiming injury. The *defendant* is the person or entity being sued. In this case there are three parties: one plaintiff, John Smith, and two defendants, Jane Doe and ABC Ambulance Service.

2.3.4 Service of the Complaint

After the complaint is filed with the court initiating the litigation process, the complaint along with a *summons* is *served* on the defendant. A summons is a legal document issued by the court commanding the defendant to appear and defend the lawsuit. This means the defendant is required to respond to the plaintiff's complaint or risk losing the case automatically. The complaint is served when a sheriff or other authorized person delivers it to the defendant. The law requires formal service to ensure that all defendants to a lawsuit receive notice of the lawsuit so that they may defend against it.

2.3.5 Defense Lawyer Retained and Answer Filed

After being served with the plaintiff's complaint, Jane Doe and ABC Ambulance retain an attorney to defend the lawsuit. The defendant's lawyer then files an *answer* with the court. The answer is the defendant's response to the plaintiff's claim and generally denies that any negligence has occurred. Exhibit 2-2 is a simplified answer for Field Incident Example 2-1.

2.3.6 Discovery

The parties to the lawsuit then enter into the *discovery* phase. Discovery primarily involves the exchange of documents and the

Exhibit 2-1 Sample Complaint

IN THE CIRCUIT COURT OF THE STATE OF TIMBUCKTOO
FOR THE COUNTY OF WHATCHAMACALLIT

JOHN SMITH,	)	
	)	
Plaintiff,	)	Case No. 89-1234
	)	
vs.	)	COMPLAINT
	)	(Negligence)
JANE DOE and ABC AMBULANCE SERVICE;	)	
	)	
Defendants.	)	

1.

Plaintiff, John Smith, is a citizen of the state of Timbucktoo residing in Whatchamacallit County.

2.

At all material times, defendant Jane Doe was and is a certified EMT-Paramedic employed by ABC Ambulance Service.

3.

At all material times, defendant ABC Ambulance Service was and is an advanced life support ambulance service licensed under the laws of the state of Timbucktoo and responsible for responding to all emergency calls within the County of Whatchamacallit.

4.

On or about July 3, 1988, ABC Ambulance responded an ambulance staffed by Jane Doe to the scene of an automobile accident involving plaintiff. After arriving at the scene, Jane Doe treated plaintiff for his injuries.

5.

In treating plaintiff's injuries, Jane Doe was negligent in failing to properly immobilize plaintiff's spine before removing him from his vehicle.

6.

As a result of Jane Doe's negligent failure to immobilize plaintiff's spine, plaintiff has been rendered a permanent quadriplegic.

Exhibit 2-1 continued

7.

As a result of Jane Doe's negligence, plaintiff has suffered damages in the amount of $_____.

WHEREFORE, plainttiff prays for judgment against defendants in the amount of $_____.

_____
Plaintiff's Lawyer

Exhibit 2-2 Sample Answer

IN THE CIRCUIT COURT OF THE STATE OF TIMBUCKTOO
FOR THE COUNTY OF WHATCHAMACALLIT

JOHN SMITH,	)	
	)	
Plaintiff,	)	Case No. 89-1234
	)	
vs.	)	ANSWER
	)	
JANE DOE and ABC AMBULANCE SERVICE;	)	
	)	
Defendants.	)	
_____	)	

1.

Defendants admit Jane Doe was a certified EMT-paramedic at the time of this incident and that ABC Ambulance Service was licensed to provide advanced life support ambulance service to Whatchamacallit County. Defendants further admit Jane Doe provided care and treatment to plaintiff on or about July 3, 1988.

2.

Except as expressly admitted, defendants deny the remainder of plaintiff's complaint and expressly deny they were negligent in any particular.

_____
Defendant's Lawyer

taking of depositions. During the early stages of litigation, each side is entitled to receive from the other all relevant documents pertaining to the suit. Thus, the plaintiff might seek documents showing the following types of information from ABC Ambulance and Jane Doe: financial information, training and continuing education courses offered employees and attended by Jane Doe, Jane Doe's personnel file, incident reports relating to the prehospital care call, medical reports relating to John Smith not already obtained, and any other important information that the defendants possess. The defendants might seek from the plaintiff all of his medical records; names of witness to the incident or to Mr. Smith's medical condition following release from the hospital; financial information showing what, if any, wage loss might be suffered by Mr. Smith as a result of his injuries; and any other important information that the plaintiff possesses.

In most states, each side also may present the other with a series of written questions relating to the lawsuit. These written questions are known as *interrogatories*. The questions are answered in consultation with the party's lawyer and then returned to the other side when completed.

Each side also is entitled to take the other's *deposition*. A deposition involves taking testimony under oath outside of a courtroom, usually in an attorney's office. During the deposition, the party is asked questions relating to the lawsuit by the other side's lawyer. Attending the deposition are each side's lawyers and a court reporter who records the questions and answers and types them up into a booklet, or *transcript*—a word-for-word account of the deposition, for later use before or during trial. The testimony given during a deposition is sworn testimony. It is testimony given just as if the party were in court. All the penalties of perjury apply in depositions as they would in court. Thus, it is important for the EMT to give a truthful and accurate account of the events as remembered. Lies or deception at deposition will be used to discredit the witness at trial. Many attorneys advise witnesses not to volunteer information and to answer each question as concisely as possible. Volunteering information may help the opposing party.

The discovery process gives each side the opportunity to fully and fairly evaluate the merits of their case. Following discovery, the case will either settle or go to trial.

2.3.7 Trial

After discovery is complete, the case goes to trial. During the trial, each side presents its side of the case. The plaintiff presents evidence first because he has the burden of proving all elements of his case. This also is known as establishing a *prima facie* case. If the plaintiff fails to establish even one element of his case, the defense wins.

Evidence is presented by witnesses who testify on two primary issues: (1) the negligence of the defendants and (2) the damages suffered by the plaintiff as a result of the defendants' negligence. In this case, the plaintiff will present expert testimony that the EMT negligently moved him from the car, which caused his quadriplegia. The plaintiff and other witnesses will testify on the effects of the injury on the plaintiff and his family.

The defendants then will present evidence. Defense experts will testify that the EMT conformed with the standard of care when moving the plaintiff. As a secondary argument, the defense will present evidence that even if the EMT were negligent, the damages are not as great as the plaintiff claims.

During trial, the judge and jury serve different functions. The judge decides issues of law—whether certain evidence should be admitted; the judge rules on objections to questioning. The jury decides the facts. For example, in Field Incident Example 2-1, Mr. Smith presented evidence that Ms. Doe extricated him from his car negligently. Ms. Doe presented evidence that she was not negligent in extricating Mr. Smith. It is the jury's role to determine which evidence to believe. Remember, if both sides agreed on the facts, there would be no need for a trial.

After both sides conclude the presentation of evidence, the jury receives instructions from the judge. These instructions, *jury instructions*, include legal definitions and legal standards that the jury must follow. The jury retires to the jury room and deliberates. The jury is only empowered to decide the facts. First, the jury must decide whether the defendants violated the standard of care. Second, if the jury finds negligent behavior, it must determine the damages the plaintiff suffered. If the jury determines that Jane Doe was not negligent, the case is concluded and Mr. Smith is not entitled to any damages. If the jury determines that Jane Doe was negligent, it must decide how much to award Mr. Smith in damages.

2.3.8 Appeal

Regardless of the outcome at trial, either side may *appeal* the decision of the trial court. An appeal is a request directed to an appellate court asking that the decision of the trial court be reviewed and changed, usually on technical legal grounds.

Before and during trial grounds for an appeal may occur. Before trial, the judge makes rulings on legal issues, such as whether the pleadings, the complaint, and the answer are proper. The judge also may rule on whether certain evidence will be allowed at trial or whether the lawyers will be allowed to argue certain matters. During trial, numerous matters arise that may influence the proceedings one way or another. How the judge rules on these matters determines whether either side may successfully appeal the trial court decision.

2.3.9 Settlement

At any point during the pendency of the lawsuit, the case may settle. Usually the EMT or the EMT's employer, through their insurance company, determines that it is best to dispose of the matter by way of settlement. In a *settlement*, the plaintiff agrees to accept some amount of money in exchange for a promise not to pursue the claim. After the case is settled, it is dismissed.

Certain cases are settled for many reasons. The insurance company and defense lawyer responsible for cases continuously monitor developments to assess defensibility and exposure. First, the chances of successfully defending the action are examined. The defense calculates the likelihood of obtaining a defense verdict and depriving the plaintiff of the ability to collect any money. Second, the likelihood of the plaintiff winning is assessed. The defense then estimates the amount of money a jury would be likely to award. These two factors are evaluated carefully to determine whether a case should settle.

More difficult to assess are those cases where the chances of successfully defending the case are fifty-fifty but the potential damage award is great. Sometimes these cases settle and sometimes they go to trial. Such assessments are made usually without much input from the EMT or the EMT's employer.

When insurance is involved, the insurance company retains the right to negotiate and settle the case. When the insurance company decides to settle the matter, the insured EMT or employer is required by the terms of the insurance contract to agree to the settlement. Again, once the case is settled, it is concluded and dismissed.

2.4 Conclusions

Understanding the law, the legal system, and the steps involved in filing and prosecuting a lawsuit is an important means of reducing fear of the legal process. The system of laws provides easy access to the courts for everyone. EMTs who understand local EMS laws are less likely to violate the law and are less likely to be involved in a lawsuit. Furthermore, EMTs who understand and comply with local EMS laws will be in a better position to defend a lawsuit should one be brought.

NOTES

1. Federal Specification KKK-A-1822B (1985): Ambulance, Emergency Medical Care Surface Vehicle.
2. Or. Rev. Stat. §823.130 (1987).
3. Or. Admin. R. 333-28-015 (1987).

Chapter *3*

Negligence

3.1 INTRODUCTION

An emergency medical technician (EMT) sitting in the kitchen of a stationhouse is paged: "EMT Smith, please report to the front desk." Upon reaching the front desk, the EMT encounters a pleasant-looking uniformed officer. After verifying the identity of the EMT, the officer hands the EMT papers. The EMT reads the papers, sweats, and contacts the supervisor who in turn contacts the agency's attorney. The EMT has been sued for negligence.

Negligence. The very word frightens many EMTs. This fear is based, in part, on a lack of knowledge about what negligence is and how the legal system processes negligence claims. The EMT feels helpless in the face of difficult-to-understand legal papers, lawyers, and a foreign language known as *legalese*.

The concept of negligence has evolved in our society into a means of governing people's actons as they relate to other people instead of "the state's" actions against people. The law of negligence provides for a mechanism that allows compensation for injuries inflicted as a result of conduct that is considered by society to be below accepted standards.

In criminal law, a person is punished for acts committed against "the state." The *state* is the governmental entity that enforces the criminal laws and prosecutes offenders of these laws. County district attorneys, state attorneys general, and federal prosecutors all represent the state in prosecuting violators of criminal laws.

In civil law, redress is permitted to put an injured person in as good a position as he or she was in before the negligent act was committed. Because the negligent action cannot be retracted nor the injury erased, the civil law has developed a means of compensating the injured victim of negligence. The person whose negligent action caused the victim's injuries is required to pay monetary damages for medical expenses, lost wages, and emotional suffering. Although such a system is not ideal, compared with other countries in which negligence is considered a criminal offense, the U.S. legal system appears to be more fair.

In this chapter, the concept of negligence, the elements of negligence, and certain defenses to negligence will be discussed. After reading this chapter, an EMT should have a better understanding of negligence and the standards of conduct expected of an EMT in the practice of the profession.

3.2 ELEMENTS OF NEGLIGENCE

In prehospital care, *negligence* can be defined as the failure to use such care as a reasonably prudent EMT would use under the same or similar circumstances; that is, conduct that falls below standards accepted by society for the protection of patients treated by EMTs. The law of negligence is founded on the concept of reasonable care in light of the circumstances of the particular case. The concept of negligence establishes a duty on the part of the EMT to exercise due care to avoid injuring a patient. Perhaps the easiest definition of negligence for an EMT to remember is that negligence simply is failure on the part of an EMT to use common sense.

Standards of conduct in negligence law are founded on a *legal fiction*. The courts have fashioned the perfect EMT—the "reasonably prudent EMT"—who always acts in accordance with society's tenets. Although no such person exists, the fictitious reasonably prudent EMT sets the standard against which the nonfictitious practicing EMT is measured. Failure to live up to this standard constitutes negligence.

The law divides negligence into four elements:

1. duty
2. breach of duty
3. causation of injury
4. damages

To win a negligence lawsuit, a person injured by an EMT must prove *each* of these four elements. If the injured person, or plaintiff, fails to prove any of these elements, he or she will lose the negligence claim.

3.2.1 Duty

The first element of negligence is *duty*. Duty is an obligation imposed by law that requires an EMT to conform to a particular standard of conduct. The EMT is required to act reasonably when performing prehospital care tasks. Examples of duties, or obligations, that apply to prehospital care personnel include

- driving carefully so that others are not endangered
- treating patients in conformance with medically recognized and accepted standards of care
- maintaining equipment in working order
- ensuring that adequate and appropriate equipment and supplies are kept in the ambulance

An EMT must act in accordance with these duties, and innumerable others, in the course of performing prehospital care tasks. It is important that an EMT recognize and understand the duties of an EMT so that he or she may avoid negligently inflicting injuries. The duty of an EMT will be measured by what a reasonably prudent EMT with similar education and training would do under the same or similar circumstances.

Field Incident Example 3-1

Facts. An EMT responds to a "person down" call at a local amusement park. After arriving at the scene, the EMT determines that an elderly male fell for no apparent reason and is complaining of head and chest pain as well as intermittent numbness down the left leg.

Question. What are some of the duties owed by the EMT to this patient?

Analysis. Before receiving a call, an EMT has a general duty to ensure that all equipment and supplies necessary to treat a patient are available in the ambulance. An EMT and the EMT's employer have an additional duty to maintain in working order all emergency equipment including, but not limited to, the cardiac monitor, defibrillator, and laryngoscope. Enroute to the scene, an EMT has a duty to drive with due regard for the safety of others. Care must be taken to avoid accidents. Upon arrival at the scene, an EMT has a duty to properly determine what treatment protocols apply to the patient and to follow these protocols appropriately.

Exercise. List other duties that apply to these facts.

An EMT owes a duty to all people with whom he or she comes in contact. Once a duty exists, it is important for an EMT to understand the nature of the duty in a particular situation. An EMT owes a duty to reasonably care for the patient. The duty to drive carefully is owed not only to the patient in the ambulance but to all other drivers and pedestrians.

Field Incident Example 3-2

Facts. An EMT is at the scene of an automobile accident in the middle of a busy intersection attempting to treat the obviously intoxicated driver of one of the cars involved. The potentially injured driver is six-foot-four, 225 pounds, and is belligerent. The injured driver is threatening to assault the driver of the other car and some of the witnesses to the accident.

Question. Does the EMT owe a duty to those people who may be injured by the belligerent driver?

Analysis. The EMT's duty toward the injured patient is clear. A duty exists to protect the patient from further injury. Additionally, the EMT owes a duty to the other driver and to the witnesses to protect them from the assault by the belligerent driver. This duty involves "securing the scene." This duty arises by virtue of the EMT's training and experience in recognizing the dangers inherent in this situation. If the EMT has a radio or other means of communication available, he or she has a duty to summon police assistance immediately. However, how far does this duty extend in terms of danger to the EMT? The law does not require that the EMT place himself or herself at risk of serious injury to protect bystanders.

EMTs often are faced with situations involving physical danger to themselves and others. Such situations may include persons with guns or knives or who seek to inflict injury on the EMT, themselves, or innocent bystanders. Although the law does not require the EMT to voluntarily place his or her own life at risk, it does impose a duty to summon law enforcement assistance as quickly as possible. Additionally, an EMT has a duty to use all reasonable means to protect patients and innocent bystanders from harm where the potential for physical violence is present.

An EMT clearly has the duty to act reasonably when the EMT is working for a prehospital care provider and is responding to a call for emergency assistance. Duty, however, is less clear in situations illustrated by Field Incident Example 3-3.

Field Incident Example 3-3

Facts. An on-duty EMT is dispatched to the residence of a chest pain patient. Enroute to the residence, the ambulance approaches the scene of a recent automobile accident with obviously injured patients.

Question. Does the EMT have a duty to stop and render assistance to the automobile accident victims or to continue to the scene of the chest pain patient?

Analysis. This situation raises complicated issues relating to the concept of duty. Once the chest pain call is accepted and the ambulance dispatched, the EMT has a duty to respond to the chest pain patient as quickly as possible to evaluate the seriousness of the patient's condition and to treat it accordingly. Once an EMT accepts a call, a duty is created toward that patient. However, no duty yet exists to the accident victims simply because the EMT drives by the accident. The EMT's duty to the cardiac patient is not eliminated by the discovery of another call, the auto accident, even though there are patients with obvious injuries. Should the EMT stop and treat the accident victims, he assumes a duty toward them and breaches his duty to the cardiac patient.

The most reasonable and prudent course of conduct is to continue to the chest pain call and to immediately radio the dispatcher to report the automobile accident and to request the immediate dispatch of another ambulance. The dispatcher has *sole authority* to alter the response. The dispatcher may reroute the first ambulance to the scene of the automobile accident and send a second ambulance to the chest pain call. If the response were altered, then the EMT's duty would be toward the auto accident victims and no longer to the chest pain patient. Should the EMT independently alter the response, he or she could be liable to the chest pain patient should injury occur.

Field Incident Example 3-3 illustrates the fact that once a duty, such as a call, is undertaken, it must be carried out in a reasonable fashion. The example also highlights the important role played by dispatchers in emergency medical services (EMS) systems. (A more detailed discussion on the dispatch function is included under 3.3.1.) Because dispatchers in EMS systems often are called on to make medically sound judgments, it is important that they are trained adequately. Some EMS systems require that dispatchers involved with EMS units be trained in accordance with standards set by the U.S. Department of Transportation.[1] Other EMS systems use the Emergency Medical Dispatch System developed by Jeff Clawson of Salt Lake City.[2]

Dispatchers often affect patient care directly. They determine what units are sent to a given call and how the community's EMS resources are allocated when multiple calls are received. The law imposes a duty on dispatchers to act responsibly when processing EMS-related calls for emergency assistance. Consider Field Incident Example 3-4.

Field Incident Example 3-4

Facts. A dispatcher receives a call from a patient complaining of chest pain (incident 1). The patient's residence is located approximately seven miles from the closest ambulance station where two advanced life support (ALS) ambulances are "in-quarters" (ambulance 1 and ambulance 2). Ambulance number 1 is dispatched. Approximately three minutes later, the dispatcher receives a radio message from ambulance 1. The ambulance has come upon the scene of an automobile accident involving serious traumatic injury to at least one occupant (incident 2). Instructions are requested.

Questions. What are the dispatcher's duties in this situation? Should ambulance 1 continue to incident 1 or stop and render aid to the automobile accident victims at incident 2? To which incident should ambulance 2 be dispatched?

Analysis. The dispatcher clearly owes a duty to the patients in both incidents to get emergency assistance to the scenes as quickly as possible. This situation presents the dispatcher with at least two choices: (1) Instruct ambulance 1 to continue to incident 1 and dispatch ambulance 2 to incident 2. (2) Instruct ambulance 1 to stop at incident 2 and dispatch ambulance 2 to incident 1.

The selection of the first choice results in a response time delay in dispatching an ambulance to incident 2, the automobile accident. Ambulance 1 is already at the accident scene and could render emergency medical care almost immediately. The decision to continue the ambulance to incident 1 will delay definitive prehospital care to the accident patient(s) until ambulance 2 is dispatched to and arrives at the accident scene.

The selection of the second choice results in a response time delay in getting an ambulance to incident 1, the cardiac emergency. The dispatcher does not know the seriousness of the patient's cardiac condition or whether cardiac arrest is imminent. Ambulance 1 is almost halfway to the cardiac patient. The decision to deter ambulance 1 to the accident scene will delay definitive prehospital care until ambulance 2 is dispatched to and arrives at the cardiac emergency scene.

No clear choices are evident and each choice could seriously harm a patient. One way to analyze Field Incident Example 3-4 is to examine it in terms of duty. The dispatcher already has undertaken a duty toward the patient in incident 1 by dispatching an ambulance to that scene. To deter the already dispatched ambulance from patient 1 may constitute a breach of that duty. Under this analysis, a decision to continue ambulance 1 to incident 1 is legally defensible. It should be remembered that once incident 2 is reported to the dispatcher, a duty arises toward the accident victims. Therefore, it is imperative that the dispatcher immediately dispatch ambulance 2 to incident 2.

Neither choice in this situation is without liability risk. Either choice is legally defensible if the dispatcher carefully analyzes the available options and makes rational decisions based on available information. Although a lawsuit may follow a dispatch delay where the delay causes injury to the patient, a jury carefully educated on the role of the dispatcher and the ramifications of each alternative choice may consider either choice reasonable and may deny damages to the plaintiff.

Another perplexing issue facing EMTs involves the existence of a legally imposed duty to aid another person when an EMT is off-duty. In examining this issue, it is important to separate the notion of a moral compulsion from legal duty.

Field Incident Example 3-5

Facts. An EMT is driving home from the local stationhouse after the EMT's shift and comes across the scene of a serious automobile accident. The EMT is in uniform and is wearing numerous patches that identify the EMT as a certified EMT–Paramedic. The EMT is driving a private car, carrying a first-aid kit with many supplies capable of assisting an automobile accident victim, and the EMT's license plate reads "I RESCUE."

Question. Does there exist a legally imposed duty on this EMT to stop and render emergency medical assistance to the victims of the automobile accident?

Analysis. If a law to the contrary does not exist, then there is no legal duty on the part of the EMT to stop and render assistance under *these* circumstances. No duty exists because the EMT in this example is a private citizen and the law does not require private citizens to aid people in peril. However, although no legal duty exists, the EMT may feel a moral or ethical obligation to stop and help the victims.

This conclusion surprises many EMTs. The fact that society does not require a medically trained person to help ill or injured individuals seems to run counter to society's notion of decency. However, the law is clear: Where no statute mandates medical assistance in off-duty situations, no *legal duty* is imposed on the EMT to help injured individuals encountered when off-duty despite the fact that an EMT may be easily identified by his or her uniform, patches, and license plate.

_____

At least two states, Vermont and Minnesota, have passed what are called *duty to rescue* laws. These laws impose a duty on the general public to aid people in distress and to grant civil immunity for all but *gross negligence* to those people rendering this aid. Gross negligence is something more than mere negligence. Gross negligence is conduct that would shock the conscience. The moving of a neck injury patient without any consideration of neck stabilization could constitute gross negligence. Specifically, the Vermont duty to rescue law states:

> A person who knows that another is exposed to grave physical harm shall, to the extent that the same can be rendered without danger or peril to himself or without interference with important duties to others, give reasonable assistance to the exposed person unless that assistance or care is being provided by others.[3]

The Minnesota duty to rescue law states:

> Any person at the scene of an emergency who knows that another person is exposed to or has suffered grave physical harm shall, to the extent that he can do so without danger or peril to himself or others, give reasonable assistance to the exposed person. Reasonable assistance may include obtaining or attempting to obtain aid from law enforcement or medical personnel.[4]

The grant of civil immunity means that an off-duty EMT who treats an injured person will not be required to pay civil damages in the event that the treatment is provided negligently. Only when the EMT is grossly negligent will he or she be liable to pay civil damages for any injuries caused by the off-duty treatment. Again, if laws contrary to those previously described do not exist, then the off-duty EMT is under no legal duty to aid people in distress.

Certain important points must be remembered regarding Field
Incident Example 3-5. Whether or not a legal duty exists, once the
EMT stops and assists the automobile accident victims, he or she
assumes a duty to act reasonably. Even though, initially, a duty to
help these patients did not exist, once the EMT begins treatment, a
legal duty exists to act as a reasonably prudent EMT under the
circumstances. Another point concerns the scope of treatment an off-
duty EMT is authorized to perform. The off-duty EMT may perform
only those tasks allowed of a basic EMT, regardless of the EMT's
actual level of certification. An off-duty EMT is not certified to act in
any advanced capacity. An EMT is permitted to perform advanced
care only under the license of a physician and only while on-duty.

The law is less clear about the duty of the EMT who works as a
volunteer. A volunteer might be on-call twenty-four hours a day,
seven days a week. Does this mean a legal duty imposes on the
volunteer the obligation to assist every ill or injured person with
whom the EMT comes in contact?

Field Incident Example 3-6

Facts. A volunteer EMT driving a private car to an office unrelated
to EMS sees an elderly individual collapse on the sidewalk. The EMT
expects a page to run this call, but has not been paged yet.

Question. Does this EMT have a duty to assist the elderly individual even before the EMT is called in as a volunteer?

Analysis. Arguably, until the EMT is paged and assumes the role
of a volunteer, no duty exists—the EMT remains a private citizen
until paged and then assumes the role of an EMT. However, if an EMT
agrees to respond to every page and is paged, then a duty clearly exists
because the EMT then is operating in an on-duty capacity. Whether a
court would impose a legal duty to act before the page would depend
on the state in which the situation arose and on the jury.

Duty, the first element of negligence, can mean different things
under different circumstances. It is important to understand the
concept of duty when an EMT is on-duty, off-duty, or when he or she
is acting as a volunteer. When there is a duty to act reasonably,
liability may follow for improperly performing that duty. Where no

duty exists in a given situation, no liability may be imposed for failing to perform that duty.

3.2.2 Breach of Duty

The second element of negligence is *breach of duty*. Once a legal duty is identified or established, breach of duty simply means the failure to conform with the standard of conduct required by that duty. In identifying a breach of duty, one must first establish what the duty is and then compare the EMT's actual conduct under the circumstances with the reasonable conduct required by that duty. Field Incident Examples 3-7, 3-8, 3-9, and 3-10 illustrate this concept.

Field Incident Example 3-7

Facts. An EMT begins a shift at 08:00. The EMT's employer requires an equipment inventory and check at the beginning of each shift. The EMT forgets to check the cardiac monitor and the monitor battery at the beginning of this shift. The first call of the day is cardiac-related and, in attempting to use the monitor, it is discovered the battery on this piece of equipment is dead.

Questions. What are the EMT's duties under the circumstances of this case? Did the EMT breach any of these duties?

Analysis. The EMT had a duty to check the battery on the cardiac monitor. This duty arises out of the employer's requirement of a daily equipment check. The failure to check the battery certainly constitutes a breach of duty.

Field Incident Example 3-8

Facts. An EMT is responding to a call using lights and siren. The EMT travels through an intersection against a red light going forty-five miles per hour and does not stop before entering the intersection.

Questions. What are the EMT's duties under the circumstances of this case? Did the EMT breach any of these duties?

Analysis. The EMT has a duty to drive his or her ambulance with due regard for the safety of others. This duty arises out of emergency vehicle operations statutes in effect nationwide. Although an EMT may be exempt from complying with certain traffic laws, there exists a duty to drive the ambulance carefully so that other drivers or pedestrians are not endangered. Driving through a controlled intersection against a red light at forty-five miles per hour without stopping to clear the intersection is definitely a breach of duty. These facts show that the EMT failed to consider the safety of others.

Field Incident Example 3-9

Facts. An EMT responds to a motor vehicle accident call. Arriving at the scene, the EMT notes a two-car accident with severe damage to both vehicles, including broken front windshields. In evaluating one patient, the EMT learns that the patient has head and neck pain and some numbness on the left side. No other injuries are noted. The patient tells the EMT that he is capable of walking to the stretcher and the EMT assists the patient to the stretcher. After lying down on the stretcher, the patient is loaded into the ambulance. No neck or spine immobilization devices are used on this patient. Local treatment protocols require that all patients with suspected neck or back injuries be placed on spine boards and that cervical collars be applied.

Questions. What are the EMT's duties under the circumstances of this case? Did the EMT breach any of these duties?

Analysis. The EMT has a duty to treat patients in conformance with medically recognized and accepted medical standards and protocols. In this case, the EMT should have suspected a neck or back injury in this patient based on the patient's complaints. At the least, the EMT had a duty to place this patient on a spine board and to apply a cervical collar. The failure to treat this patient in conformance with the local protocols is a breach of duty toward this patient.

Field Incident Example 3-10

Facts. In checking the ambulance at the beginning of the shift, an EMT fails to inventory the intravenous supplies and thus fails to note the absence of certain intravenous fluids. The EMT later responds to a call involving a patient with multiple system trauma from a fall and is unable to begin fluid therapy because the appropriate intravenous fluids are unavailable.

Questions. What are the EMT's duties under the circumstances of this case? Did the EMT breach any of these duties?

Analysis. The EMT has a duty to ensure that adequate and appropriate equipment and supplies are kept in the ambulance. The failure to inventory and resupply the intravenous supplies constitutes a breach of duty.

———

In analyzing any situation, it is important for the EMT to first identify what duty or duties apply to the given situation. Then, the actual conduct of the EMT is compared with the identified duties to determine whether a breach of duty occurred.

In reviewing the preceding examples, keep in mind that whether any liability will follow from the breach of duty depends on whether the breach of duty resulted in injury to the patient.

3.2.3 Causation of Injury

The third element the plaintiff must prove to win a negligence lawsuit is *causation of injury*. In addition to duty and breach of duty, the plaintiff must prove that the EMT's failure to conform to the standard of conduct required under the circumstances resulted in the plaintiff's injury. An EMT is not responsible legally for any preexisting injury or illness. However, an EMT may be liable for exacerbating an injury or causing additional injury. The causal link between the EMT's negligence and the plaintiff's injury must be direct and traceable. Field Incident Examples 3-11 and 3-12 explore the element of causation.

———

Field Incident Example 3-11

Facts. An EMT, in treating a motor vehicle accident victim with highly suspicious signs of a neck injury fails to immobilize the patient's neck and spine. Before being moved to the stretcher and transported, the patient has full feeling and mobility in all extremities. Upon arrival at the hospital, the patient can no longer feel or move the lower extremities.

Question. Assuming that the EMT breached a legal duty in this situation, is the element of causation of injury provable in these circumstances?

Analysis. Here, there is a direct causal connection between the EMT's breach of duty in failing to immobilize the patient's neck and the resulting spinal cord injury. The plaintiff automobile accident patient could prove that the EMT's conduct caused the plaintiff's paralysis. The patient in this example fractured a cervical spine at the time of the accident. The EMT is not responsible for causing this initial fracture. Instead, the EMT is responsible for those injuries because of the EMT's breach of duty toward this patient—spinal cord damage resulting from failure to immobilize the patient's neck.

Field Incident Example 3-12

Facts. An EMT responds to a "person down" call in front of a local supermarket. On arrival, the EMT finds a patient who reportedly fell and was unconscious for approximately five minutes. Exam reveals a conscious and alert female, oriented to time, place, and person and who shows no obvious injuries and has no other complaints except a headache. The EMT, who consults with the patient, determines that the patient does not need to obtain further medical attention. (Assume for purposes of this example that a more careful examination would have led the EMT to conclude that the patient should be evaluated further by a physician. Assume also that the patient would have permitted transport to the hospital had the EMT encouraged it.) As a result of injuries sustained from the original fall, the patient later becomes dizzy at home, falls a second time, and strikes her head on the corner of a countertop. This second fall causes further head injuries from the effects of which the patient dies.

Question. Assuming the EMT breached a legal duty in this situation, is the element of causation of injury provable in these circumstances?

Analysis. Although the causal link is more difficult to trace in this situation, the element of causation of injury still is present. Here, the plaintiff must prove that the injuries sustained in the first fall contributed to the second fall and resulting death. Had the EMT properly determined the seriousness of the first head injury and transported the patient to the hospital, the second fall probably would not have occurred. Thus, the EMT caused this death by unreasonably releasing the patient.

A plaintiff must prove all four elements of negligence to prevail in a negligence lawsuit. However, a plaintiff who proves that an EMT breached a duty but fails to prove that the breach of duty resulted in injury cannot be successful in bringing a claim for negligence. Consider Field Incident Examples 3-13 and 3-14.

Field Incident Example 3-13

Facts. A paramedic unit responds to a cardiac arrest call. The EMTs fail to follow the cardiac arrest protocol in that they improperly and inadequately perform cardiopulmonary resuscitation (CPR). The patient dies. The medical evidence gathered after the call shows that regardless of what the EMTs did or failed to do, the patient would not have survived.

Question. Assuming the EMT breached a legal duty in this situation, is the element of causation of injury provable in these circumstances?

Analysis. The case illustrates an example of the absence of the element of causation. The EMT clearly breached a duty to this patient by failing to properly follow the cardiac arrest protocol. However, nothing the EMT could have done would have saved the patient's life. Thus, the plaintiff cannot show that the EMT's negligence resulted in the patient's death. Regardless of how poorly the EMT performed, there is no liability for this outcome.

Field Incident Example 3-14

Facts. An ambulance, responding with lights and siren, travels through an intersection against a red light at ninety miles per hour. No collision occurs between the ambulance and any other vehicle.

Question. Assuming the EMT breached a legal duty in this situation, is the element of causation of injury provable in these circumstances?

Analysis. This is another example of what is sometimes called "negligence in the air." Here, the EMT clearly breached the duty to drive with due regard for the safety of others by recklessly driving the "hot" ambulance through the intersection. This breach of duty, however, did not result in injury to anyone. Thus, no liability follows for this substandard conduct.

In the prehospital care setting, the element of causation of injury is often the stumbling block to a plaintiff pursuing or successfully winning a negligence claim. Often, showing that an EMT breached a duty toward a potential plaintiff is fairly easy. However, as the preceding examples illustrate, it may be impossible to show that the EMT's breach of duty resulted in any injury to the patient. The absence of any of the four elements of negligence, including causation of injury, can keep the plaintiff from successfully recovering damages. Case Summary 3-1 highlights this point.

Case Summary 3-1

Case Citation. Gianechini v. City of New Orleans, 410 So.2d 292 (La. 1982).

Facts. Plaintiff, Mrs. Gianechini, brought a wrongful death action on behalf of her deceased husband. She claimed that City of New Orleans fire fighters negligently rendered emergency cardiac care resulting in her husband's death.

Mr. Gianechini suffered a heart attack at a restaurant. A bystander, an off-duty paramedic, and another person, identified as a doctor, immediately began CPR. Within three to five minutes, an emergency vehicle staffed by the defendant fire fighters arrived. The fire fighters began administering emergency aid and continued administering aid during transport to the hospital. The plaintiff claimed that the fire fighters negligently performed CPR resulting in the death of her husband; that is, the plaintiff claimed that proper CPR would have saved her husband's life. A jury ruled in favor of the city and the plaintiff appealed.

Court Ruling. Because of a Louisiana immunity law, the plaintiff was required to prove that one of the fire fighters was *grossly* negligent, not just merely negligent. The jury found no gross negligence on the part of the fire fighters and the appeals court agreed. More importantly, the appeals court concluded that the plaintiff had failed to prove that proper CPR would have made a difference in outcome. Nothing the fire fighter/EMTs could have done would have prevented Mr. Gianechini's death. Thus, the fire fighters and city were not liable.

Analysis. In this case the appeals court focused, in part, on the element of causation to uphold the jury's verdict in favor of the City of New Orleans. The court recognized that the plaintiff failed to establish a causal link between the fire fighter's conduct and the decedent's death. Thus, the plaintiff failed to prove the important causation-of-injury requirement of her negligence claim and could not recover damages for the death of her husband.

3.2.4 Damages

The fourth and final element the plaintiff must prove to win a negligence claim is that of damages. The plaintiff must show an actual loss or damage for which the law allows recovery. Where physical injury results from an EMT's negligence, actual damages usually are proven easily. Damages are divided into two general categories: (1) *compensatory* or actual damages and (2) *punitive* damages. Both of these types of damages may be sought against an EMT in instances in which the EMT's breach of duty results in injury to a person.

Compensatory damages are designed to compensate the injured party for the injury sustained as a result of the EMT's breach of duty. This category of damages is divided into subcategories of *special* and *general* damages. Special damages include those items that are easily quantifiable or provable. Examples of special damages include lost wages, medical expenses, and property damage resulting from the EMT's breach of duty. General damages are less quantifiable but may result from an EMT's substandard performance in treating a patient. Examples of general damages include pain and suffering, emotional distress, and the loss of the companionship on the part of the injured party and the injured party's family.

Punitive damages are designed to punish the defendant and to set an example for others who may engage in similar conduct. Usually, the conduct giving rise to an award of punitive damages is much more severe than simple negligence. Although punitive damages rarely are awarded in prehospital care cases, certain situations may warrant punitive damages. For example, punitive damages may be awarded against the driver of the ambulance who runs a red light at ninety miles per hour (Field Incident Example 3-14) and then collides with another car, which results in serious injury or death.

When the plaintiff proves that a breach of duty resulted in injury, it usually is easy to show at least some compensatory damages. The necessity of an award of punitive damages is more difficult to prove.

3.3 ADDITIONAL EXAMPLES OF NEGLIGENCE CONCEPTS

In the course of a career, an EMT likely will encounter innumerable prehospital care field incidents. Several prehospital care incidents are explored in this section in the context of negligence law.

By learning to apply the legal principles learned using this book to specific EMS situations, an EMT will be better able to assess the litigation potential of any given situation. An understanding of the potential legal ramifications of alternative courses of action will help an EMT act reasonably in treating patients, thus avoiding the possibility of a lawsuit. For example, an EMT who is aware of the duty to drive an ambulance with due regard for the safety of others may operate an ambulance more carefully. This knowledge and resulting carefulness should reduce the likelihood of an accident and thereby reduce the potential for litigation.

In reading this section, keep in mind the concept of duty. In essence, every lawsuit flows from a breach of duty. The law imposes an obligation or duty on an EMT to act in conformance with acceptable medical practices when treating victims of particular prehospital care incidents. An understanding of the nature of an EMT's duty in a given situation will help an EMT meet those obligations. In the prehospital field situations discussed, the issue of duty is the primary focus of analysis. In reviewing these examples, consider other duties that also may apply to the situations.

3.3.1 Dispatch

The dispatch function is an important component of any EMS system. EMS dispatchers, as EMS professionals, play an important role in receiving calls for emergency assistance, sending appropriate EMS units, and allocating EMS resources when multiple calls are received by the system. The duties of EMS dispatchers are numerous. The dispatcher has a duty to use correct radio procedures, to obtain correct information from the calling party in a timely fashion, to screen calls appropriately, and to dispatch appropriate resources to the scene of a medical emergency. The breach of any of these duties that results in injury to the patient may result in a negligence claim.

Case Summary 3-2

Case Citation. *Letter v. City of Portland*, No. A8405-03063 (Multnomah County Or. Cir. Ct. July 24, 1986). [Unreported trial court case.]

Facts. The plaintiff awoke and discovered a burglar in her apartment. Just prior to the burglar's attack, the plaintiff managed to dial 911 and had a brief opportunity to report the nature and location of her emergency. The dispatcher answered the call according to standard operating procedure, saying "police, fire, or medical?" As a result of the dispatcher's talking, the plaintiff was unable to report her address. The plaintiff was unable to complete the call because of a sexual assault; the line remained open.

The plaintiff sued the city of Portland, claiming that the dispatch operator was negligent in interrupting her and failing to properly record her address. She claimed that at least some of her injuries could have been prevented if the police had been dispatched in a timely fashion.

Court Ruling. A jury, after hearing the evidence, awarded the plaintiff $120,000 in damages against the city, finding negligence on the part of the dispatcher.

Analysis. This case highlights a dispatcher's important duty to properly obtain and record a calling party's address. By definition, a dispatcher will be dealing constantly with lay people facing emergency situations who may be panicked.

Case Summary 3-3

Case Citation. *Trezzi v. City of Detroit*, 120 Mich. App. 506, 328 N.W.2d 70 (1983).

Facts. This case involves the operation of a police 911 emergency dispatch system. Operators at the 911 center, in the normal course of their duties, generally attach priority ratings to each call based upon its nature. Police units then are dispatched in accordance with the priority rating.

The plaintiff sued the city of Detroit as operator of the 911 system, claiming that several 911 calls were made to the dispatch center requesting emergency police assistance. (The reason for the emergency calls is not detailed in the case.) The plaintiff, representing deceased relatives, also claimed that the 911 operators attached an unjustifiably low priority rating to these calls, which resulted in a 1½-hour delay before police units were dispatched to the scene. As a result of this delay, the plaintiff's relatives sustained numerous injuries from which they died.

Court Ruling. This case addressed primarily the issue of governmental immunity. The city of Detroit asked the court to dismiss the plaintiff's claim because the city was immune from liability on certain technical legal grounds. The court agreed and dismissed the plaintiff's case. Therefore, the nature of the 911 center's duties was not explored in detail by the court.

Analysis. Although this case was dismissed on governmental immunity grounds, it highlights several dispatcher duties as they apply to EMS. The plaintiff claimed that dispatchers have a duty to correctly assign priority ratings to calls received to ensure emergency units are dispatched in a timely fashion. EMS dispatchers have a similar duty. If multiple calls come into a dispatch center simultaneously, EMS dispatchers have a duty to correctly prioritize those calls and to dispatch units in a timely fashion. When emergency units in the EMS system are depleted by numerous calls, the dispatcher has a duty to allocate calls based on the nature of the emergencies and to call in units from outside the area, if necessary. An unjustifiable delay in dispatching EMS vehicles to the scene of a medical emergency may result in litigation where the delay causes injury to the patient.

3.3.2 Patient Care Capabilities

It is important that appropriate resources be dispatched to the scene of a medical emergency. In an EMS system with basic and advanced capabilities, advanced life support (ALS) vehicles should be sent on ALS calls and basic life support (BLS) vehicles should be sent on BLS calls. Both the dispatcher and the responding unit have a duty. The dispatcher must screen the calls appropriately and send vehicles with appropriate capabilities. The EMTs in the responding units must recognize when a particular incident is beyond their own capabilities and request additional help. The BLS crew attempting to treat an ALS patient when an ALS ambulance is close by and available clearly breaches its duty toward the patient. Case Summary 3-4 examines this duty.

Case Summary 3-4

Case Citation. Brooks v. Herndon Ambulance Service, Inc., 475 So.2d 1319 (Fla. App. 5th Dist. 1985).

Facts. The plaintiff, representing her deceased son, brought a wrongful death action against Herndon Ambulance Service claiming, among other things, that a BLS ambulance was dispatched to an ALS call although an ALS ambulance was a short distance away. The plaintiff claimed that the delay in receiving ALS care resulted in the son's death.

The plaintiff's son suffered a sudden onset of convulsions, anoxia, fibrillation, and cardiac arrest while participating in his high school physical education class. Herndon Ambulance Service, the exclusive franchise provider of ambulance service to the area, was summoned and dispatched a BLS ambulance to the scene. The plaintiff claimed that a local fire department had ALS units available within a short distance but that none of these units was called despite Herndon's own policies to the contrary. The plaintiff further claimed that the failure to dispatch personnel and equipment capable of providing ALS care resulted in her son's death.

Court Ruling. At Herndon's request, the trial court dismissed the plaintiff's claims on technical legal grounds. The appeals court reversed the trial court's ruling, saying that the plaintiff's claims, if proven, should be decided by a jury.

Analysis. This case points out the importance of dispatching appropriate EMS units to particular calls. When ALS and BLS vehicles are available to respond to a call, the dispatcher has a duty to send ALS ambulances to calls potentially involving life-threatening emergencies. The dispatch of emergency vehicles with improper capabilities may result in litigation where the failure to dispatch ALS units results in patient injury or death. The crew in a responding ambulance also may be liable for failing to request the dispatch of an ALS ambulance. The crew has a duty to recognize when a patient requires ALS care and to provide that care if available. In this case, ALS capabilities clearly were available, but were not used.

3.3.3 Driving/Vehicular Liability

The driver of an emergency vehicle owes a duty to other drivers, pedestrians, and bicyclists who may be injured as a result of negligent emergency vehicle operation. Most states have laws governing the operation of emergency vehicles. An EMT who violates these laws may be found negligent despite the circumstances of the emergency. The EMT/driver should know all relevant state laws and the general duty to drive with due regard for the safety of others.

Most states have statutes that set forth the duties of drivers of emergency vehicles. These emergency vehicle operations statutes use similar language imposing on emergency vehicle operators the obligation to drive with the safety of others in mind. Consider the following section of the Montana statute, which is representative of this type of law nationwide.

§61-8-107 . . . [A]uthorized emergency vehicles.

(1) The driver of a[n] . . . authorized emergency vehicle, when responding to an emergency call . . . may exercise the privileges set forth in this section, but subject to the conditions herein stated.

(2) The driver of a[n] . . . emergency vehicle may: . . .

(a) proceed past a red or stop signal or stop sign, but only after slowing down as may be necessary for safe operation;

(b) exceed the speed limits so long as he does not endanger life or property;

(c) disregard regulations governing direction of movement or turning in specified directions.

(3) The exemptions granted to a[n] . . . authorized emergency vehicle apply only when the vehicle is making use of audible or visual signal, or both. . . .

(4) *The foregoing provisions shall not relieve the driver of a[n] . . . authorized emergency vehicle from the duty to drive with due regard for the safety of all persons, nor shall such provisions protect the driver from the consequences of his reckless disregard for the safety of others.* [Emphasis added.]⁵

Montana's statute, like almost all others, exempts the driver of an ambulance from certain traffic laws but imposes on the EMT the duty to drive carefully when exercising this privilege. If an EMT carries out this duty, no liability will follow even if an accident occurs. Consider the Case Summary 3-5 and Field Incident Examples 3-15 and 3-16.

Case Summary 3-5

Case Citation. Rohrkaste v. City of Terre Haute, 470 N.E.2d 738 (Ind. App. 3d Dist. 1984).

Facts. An ambulance owned by the city of Terre Haute, Indiana, collided with an automobile driven by the plaintiff as the ambulance traveled through a red light at an intersection. The ambulance's siren and lights were in use at the time of the accident. The plaintiff sued the city for the resulting personal injuries and for property damage.

Court Ruling. A jury returned a verdict in favor of the city, finding no liability on the part of the ambulance driver. The plaintiff appealed on a number of grounds. The court of appeals concluded that the jury's verdict was proper, in part because the trial court had correctly instructed the jury on the law of emergency vehicle operations. Therefore, the verdict in favor of the city was allowed to stand.

Analysis. The portion of this case addressing emergency vehicle operations statutes and the general vehicle code contrasted the duty of the driver of an automobile when an emergency vehicle approaches with that of the operator of an emergency vehicle. The driver of an automobile has a duty to yield the right-of-way to an emergency vehicle displaying flashing lights and giving audible warning signals by siren. Like the Montana emergency vehicle operations statute, Indiana imposes the duty on the driver of an ambulance to act with due regard for the safety of others. The jury, having heard all the evidence on these contrasting duties, found the ambulance driver to have acted reasonably. Therefore, no liability followed.

Field Incident Example 3-15

Facts. The driver of an ambulance approaches an intersection controlled by four-way stop signs. The driver uses emergency lights but no siren. It is 3:00 A.M. and there is little traffic. The driver slows from fifty-five miles per hour and travels through the intersection at forty miles per hour. The ambulance strikes a bicyclist whom the ambulance driver did not see. Serious injury results.

Question. Did this ambulance driver perform with due regard for the safety of others?

Analysis. The driver of this ambulance had a duty to drive carefully so not to injure others. Such a duty imposes an obligation to use the siren as well as the emergency lights to warn both automobile and pedestrian traffic of the ambulance's presence. There exists an additional duty to slow to a safe speed before proceeding through a controlled intersection. This driver failed to act reasonably in both respects.

Traveling without an audible siren violates the standard of care because it fails to provide adequate warning to pedestrians and other drivers. Traveling through any controlled intersection at any time at excessive speed is reckless and certainly violates the standard of care. Although the bicyclist may be at fault to at least some degree, the primary responsibility for the accident rests with the driving EMT.

The duties imposed on drivers of EMS vehicles are obvious to most EMTs. Most accidents involving ambulances are avoidable. The EMT can avert litigation problems by using common sense and by driving carefully.

3.3.4 Equipment Failure/Maintenance

EMTs have a duty to check the equipment in their ambulance at the beginning of every shift and after every use. Failure to do so may lead to a negligence claim. An example of equipment failure resulting from EMT neglect is a dead battery on a defibrillator. The patient who cannot be cardioverted because of this negligence, or more likely the patient's family, probably will file a negligence claim against the EMT who failed to check the battery.

Similarly, emergency services have a duty to maintain emergency vehicles and equipment in working order. A breach of this duty, which results in patient injury, may lead to a negligence claim. The emergency service that fails to regularly check the brakes on emergency vehicles leaves itself open to a lawsuit. The patient who is injured when the emergency vehicle is involved in an accident because it could not stop will look to the emergency service for compensation.

Field Incident Example 3-16

Facts. An EMT notes problems with the brakes on an ambulance and reports these problems to the service's supervisor. The supervisor instructs the EMT to continue to use the ambulance to run calls because the brakes were checked recently. The EMT, fearful of employer retaliation for refusing to drive the ambulance, complies and accepts the next call dispatched. Because of the brake problem, the ambulance is involved in an accident that results in injury to a patient.

Question. Are the EMT and emergency service provider liable to pay damages to the patient injured in this accident?

Analysis. The EMT initially complied with the duty to report an equipment malfunction. However, once having discovered the brake defect in the ambulance, the EMT owed an additional duty to all who might be injured *not* to drive the impaired ambulance. The EMT breached this duty by accepting the next call and is liable to anyone injured by the defective ambulance. That the supervisor instructed the EMT to drive the ambulance is not a good excuse or justification for the conduct.

The emergency service similarly is liable in this example. Once having been notified of the brake problem, the supervisor had a duty to take the ambulance out of service. A further duty then is imposed to have the ambulance inspected and repaired by a qualified mechanic. The instruction to continue to operate an ambulance with *known* brake problems constitutes particularly egregious conduct perhaps rising to the level of *gross* negligence warranting the award of punitive damages.

The best way to avoid problems relating to equipment failure is to conduct regular equipment checks. EMS providers should provide checklists to employees to ensure that all equipment is evaluated on a regular basis. Mechanic's logs also should be maintained as documentation of the provider's maintenance activities.

Many times equipment will fail as a result of a defect in the apparatus itself rather than any neglect on the part of the EMT or the EMS provider. In a lawsuit, however, the onus may be on the prehospital care provider to show that the equipment failure did not result from the EMS provider's negligence.

3.3.5 Spinal Cord Injuries

Because the potential injuries resulting from improper care are so serious, EMTs who respond to the aid of a spinal cord injury patient must be particularly careful. A motor vehicle accident victim who has spinal subluxation and is moved improperly may suffer permanent and severe injuries. The EMT, therefore, owes a duty to this patient to move the patient slowly, carefully applying neck immobilization devices when appropriate. The patient who suffers permanent paralysis as a result of EMT negligence is likely to bring a lawsuit seeking substantial damages.

3.3.6 Emotionally Disturbed Patients

The emotionally disturbed patient presents difficult problems for the prehospital care provider. The EMT must recognize the abnormal nature of the patient's behavior and treat accordingly. An emotionally disturbed patient's behavior may be affected by a number of factors, including mental illness, medical illness, suicidal tendencies, or drug and alcohol abuse. In treating such patients, the EMT must exercise caution to avoid injury to the patient, bystanders, and the EMT. For example, the EMT has a duty not to abandon the suicidal patient or the medically ill diabetic patient. Similarly, the EMT has a duty to prevent injury caused by drug- or alcohol-induced violence. Potential injury to the EMT, of course, will be considered in such situations. Most importantly, the EMT has a duty to recognize the factors that contribute to the patient's condition under circumstances in which the patient may either be unable or unwilling to cooperate.

3.3.7 Law Enforcement Involvement in EMS

Many prehospital care incidents and scenes involve the presence of law enforcement personnel. Questions arise regarding the duties and responsibilities of each of these emergency responders. Key issues revolve around patient care decision-making authority, patient restraint, crime scene control, and crime reporting.

Generally, when both emergency medical and law enforcement personnel are involved in a prehospital care incident, the EMT is responsible for patient care and the law enforcement officer is responsible for public safety. Patient care decision-making authority remains with the EMT. In most states, EMTs do not have the authority to physically restrain patients—only law enforcement officers have such authority.

Law enforcement involvement in EMS may create many legal pitfalls for an EMT. An EMT who gives a law enforcement officer patient care decision-making authority may face a negligence claim against the EMT.

Field Incident Example 3-17

Facts. An ALS unit responds to a jail on a "man down" call. Upon arrival, the EMTs find an inmate complaining of severe headaches and dizziness. Suspecting serious head injury, they determine that the patient should be seen in the local emergency department. The responsible officers tell the EMTs that further treatment is not necessary because the patient has faked illnesses previously. The EMTs accept this explanation and leave without insisting upon further examination or treatment for this patient. The patient later dies from a brain hemorrhage. A negligence claim against the EMTs most likely will follow.

Question. Are the EMTs liable to pay damages for the injuries sustained by the patient?

Analysis. The most prudent course of action for the EMTs is to transport the patient to the hospital. If law enforcement personnel seek to refuse medical treatment on the patient's behalf, then the EMTs should contact medical control if available. An on-line physician may be able to persuade the officers to allow the patient to be transported. If on-line medical control is unavailable and the officers refuse to allow transport, the EMTs should document the incident extensively and report the events to their supervisor.

In many EMS systems it is common for law enforcement officers to cancel responding ambulances before they arrive at the scene of an emergency call. Such a practice is dangerous and may result in a successful lawsuit against the EMS provider as well as the police agency. If police officers who are not medically trained make medical decisions, liability may follow. If, for example, a patient in an automobile accident fails to obtain needed medical attention because a first-arriving police officer cancels the responding ambulance, the patient may sue. The police agency may be liable for having a policy that allows the cancellation of an ambulance by persons who are not medically trained. The EMS provider may be liable for following the untrained officer's instructions. Policies must be crafted to ensure that law enforcement personnel do not intercede in the medical decision-making process.

3.4 NEGLIGENCE: CONCLUSIONS

In a negligence lawsuit, the plaintiff must prove all four elements of a negligence claim: (1) duty, (2) breach of duty, (3) causation of injury, and (4) damages. An EMT who fails to act reasonably toward a particular person or who fails to conform to a particular standard of conduct breaches a duty toward that person. However, the plaintiff also must show a causal connection between the substandard conduct and the injury and that actual damages were sustained. A plaintiff who proves all of these elements can recover damages from the EMT.

3.5 DEFENSES TO A NEGLIGENCE CLAIM

A *defense* to a lawsuit is defined as a legal or factual reason why the plaintiff should not be entitled to some or all of the damages claimed.

A defense may act as a partial or complete limitation on the plaintiff's right to collect damages even though the plaintiff's claim is valid. In a lawsuit, the plaintiff may be correct in his assertion that an EMT's negligence resulted in serious injury. However, if a defendant successfully raises a defense, the plaintiff may be prohibited from pursuing the claim or from collecting some or all of the damages awarded by a jury or court.

A plaintiff files a lawsuit against a defendant EMT claiming that the EMT negligently caused injury to the plaintiff. The defendant's attorney determines what, if any, defenses may apply to the facts of the given case. Some defenses are raised early in the litigation process and are decided by a judge while others are decided later, at trial, by a jury. Examples of defenses to negligence claims include

- Good Samaritan laws
- immunity statutes
- statutes of limitation
- comparative/contributory negligence
- governmental immunity

Each of these defenses to negligence claims is discussed. The successful application of any of these defenses may reduce or eliminate the plaintiff's right to collect damages from the EMT.

3.5.1 Good Samaritan Laws

A *Good Samaritan* is defined as a person who compassionately gives personal assistance to another person. Under certain circumstances, Good Samaritan laws protect these Good Samaritans from having to pay civil damages. Within the context of these laws, an individual who aids another in imminent and serious peril cannot be held liable for injuries suffered by the victim as a result of the rescuer's conduct. The policy behind these laws is to encourage people to help others in need without fear of liability consequences. All states now have some form of a Good Samaritan law, some of which may apply to EMTs.

EMTs often ask whether they are obligated by law to help ill or injured persons when the EMTs are off-duty. A follow-up question is whether Good Samaritan laws protect the off-duty EMT who does render assistance. The answers to these questions vary somewhat from state to state but certain general principles apply nationwide. It is important for the EMT to understand that Good Samaritan laws, where applicable, act as a defensive shield in a lawsuit.

An off-duty EMT generally is under *no legal duty* to stop and render assistance unless the state has a duty to rescue law. For purposes of this discussion, assume that no such law exists. Remember, however, that once the off-duty EMT stops and aids a victim, he or she must act as a reasonably prudent person with the training and experience of a similar EMT under similar circumstances. Normally, liability will follow if the EMT acts negligently. However, if a Good Samaritan law protects the EMT, there is no liability even if the EMT acted negligently.

The protection afforded by Good Samaritan laws varies. To obtain protection, the EMT must meet the legal criteria in the EMT's state. The following elements of Good Samaritan laws are found throughout the United States; however, not all of these elements are found in every state's Good Samaritan law:

- *protected class* requirement
- *good faith* requirement
- *without expectation of compensation* requirement
- *location* requirement
- *minimum standard of conduct* requirement

In seeking the protection of this type of law, *all* requirements of the state's Good Samaritan law must be met. First, the EMT must be a member of the class of persons protected by the law. A protected class is a group of persons intended by the state's legislature to receive immunity under the particular statute. Protected classes can include physicians, nurses, police officers, fire fighters, EMTs, and paramedics. Some states provide protection to "any person." If the EMT is a member of the listed class, the first element is met.

A state's Good Samaritan law may require that assistance be given in good faith. Good Samaritan laws generally do not define the term good faith, which denotes an abstract and intangible quality usually meaning the absence of malice. In a given case, a jury probably would be left to decide whether an EMT acted in good faith when he or she rendered off-duty assistance.

The next element of many Good Samaritan laws requires that the EMT act without expectation of compensation; that is, the EMT cannot receive compensation for performing the emergency service. This element arguably removes many volunteers from Good Samaritan law protection because the receipt of a uniform or equipment is a form of compensation. Thus, a volunteer may be exempt from protection. This issue of the uncompensated volunteer is not resolved easily. Whether a volunteer who receives no compensation would be protected by a given Good Samaritan law would depend on how the state interpreted the without expectation of compensation requirement. Generally, though, an off-duty EMT is protected.

Some Good Samaritan laws require the care in question be given at a certain location. For example, some laws require that emergency assistance be rendered "at the scene of the emergency" or "outside the hospital." The EMT who provides emergency care in a location outside the scope of the law will not receive the protection of the Good Samaritan law.

The most critical element of any Good Samaritan law and the most difficult to understand relates to the minimum standard of conduct required. Varying standards of conduct described in Good Samaritan laws denote the type of conduct not protected. The range of standards of conduct includes negligent, grossly negligent, reckless, willful, wanton, and intentional. Whether the law provides *any* protection to an EMT who renders emergency medical assistance depends in large part on the delineated standard. Consider that the EMT is immune from liability *unless* he or she acts in a [insert standard of conduct] manner.

If the standard described is negligence, which represents the least worst form of conduct, then the law provides *no* protection. If an EMT acts reasonably and meets the standard of care, there is no need for Good Samaritan-law protection because there is no liability for rendering reasonable care. However, if an EMT acts negligently, he or she may seek Good Samaritan-law protection. If the law does not provide immunity for negligent conduct, the law will not protect the EMT who acts negligently. Thus, no immunity will apply and the patient may seek compensation from the EMT.

If the standard described in the Good Samaritan law is worse than negligence, such as gross negligence or intentional conduct, the EMT may be immune from paying damages for merely negligent conduct. If the law states that the EMT is immune from paying civil damages unless he or she acts intentionally, Good Samaritan-law protection will apply to the EMT who acts negligently.

The following is a hypothetical example of a Good Samaritan law. Note that information in brackets refers to the elements of a Good Samaritan law: 1-protected class requirement, 2-good faith requirement, 3-without expectation of compensation requirement, 4-location requirement, and 5-minimum standard of conduct requirement.

[Any person][1] [who in good faith][2] and [without expectation of compensation][3] renders emergency medical assistance to a patient [at the scene of an emergency][4] is not liable to pay civil damages for any act or omission that occurs in connection with the services or treatment rendered [if the services or treatment are performed in a non-negligent manner.][5]

This hypothetical law provides virtually no protection to the EMT because the standard of the law is one of negligence. Remember: The EMT who acts reasonably and, therefore, non-negligently, does not need Good Samaritan-law protection. This sample law does not protect negligent care and, thus, deprives a Good Samaritan EMT of protection for negligence even if the EMT meets all other requirements of the law. A jury in many cases will decide if an EMT's conduct was negligent, grossly negligent, or worse.

Exercise 3-1

Facts. A California law states that

No person who in good faith, and not for compensation, renders emergency care at the scene of an emergency shall be liable for any civil damages resulting from any act or omission. The scene of an emergency shall not include emergency departments and other places where medical care is usually offered.[6]

Exercise. Analyze each element of this California law and determine the level of Good Samaritan protection provided.

————————•

3.5.2 Immunity Statutes

In addition to laws that provide Good Samaritan-law protection to EMTs and other people who meet the requirements of the law, immunity statutes have been enacted by some states. These laws are designed to protect prehospital care providers from having to pay civil damages for acts performed on-the-job. Such laws are analyzed in the same way as Good Samaritan laws: The EMT must meet each element of an immunity statute including the standard of conduct requirement.

Exercise 3-2

Facts. A Massachusetts law provides as follows:

> No emergency medical technician . . . who in the performance of his duties and in good faith renders emergency first aid or transportation to an injured person or to a person incapacitated by illness shall be personally in any way liable as a result of rendering such aid or as a result of transporting such person to a hospital or other safe place. . . .[7]

Exercise. Analyze each element of this immunity statute as you did for Exercise 3-1 and determine the level of protection provided and the standard or standards of conduct protected by this law.

Exercise 3-3

Facts. A Texas law provides as follows:

> Any individual, agency, organization, institution, corporation, or entity of state or local government that authorizes, sponsors, supports, finances, or supervises the functions of . . . emergency medical services personnel is not liable for any civil damages for any act or omission that occurs in connection with . . . any part of the services or treatment rendered to a patient or potential patient by emergency medical services personnel, if the . . . services or treatment are performed in accordance with the standard of ordinary care.[8]

Exercise. Analyze each element of this immunity statute and determine the level of protection provided and the standard or standards of conduct protected by this law.

_____

Exercise 3-4

Facts. A California law provides as follows:

> [I]n order to encourage the provision of emergency medical services by firefighters, police officers or other law enforcement officers, EMT-I, EMT-II or EMT-P, a firefighter, police officer or other law enforcement officer, EMT-I, EMT-II or EMT-P who renders emergency medical services at the scene of an emergency shall only be liable in civil damages for acts or omissions performed in a grossly negligent manner or acts or omissions not performed in good faith. . . .[9]

Exercise. Analyze each element of this immunity statute and determine the level of protection provided and the standard or standards of conduct protected by this law.

_____

Immunity statutes and Good Samaritan laws are similar except for the no expectation of compensation requirement. They differ, however, in that immunity statutes for emergency care providers do not exist in most states, but Good Samaritan laws are present in every state, although not every state provides Good Samaritan-law protection to prehospital care providers.

An EMT should analyze carefully his or her state's Good Samaritan and immunity statutes to determine what is required to achieve civil liability protection from these laws. Specific questions about these laws should be directed to the EMT's supervisor or to the provider's attorney.

3.5.3 Statutes of Limitation

Another defense to a negligence claim involves *statutes of limitation*, which are statutory time limits placed on the right of an individual to bring a lawsuit. The main purpose of these laws is to require the filing of claims in a timely manner while memories are vivid and witnesses are available. Consider Field Incident Example 3-18.

Field Incident Example 3-18

Facts. In January 1984, an EMT committed a negligent act that resulted in injury to a patient. The particular state's law provided that a lawsuit for negligence had to be brought within two years of the date of negligent treatment. The patient sued the EMT in February 1986.

Question. Could the patient successfully collect damages from the EMT because the EMT's negligence resulted in injury to the patient?

Analysis. No, because the lawsuit was brought after the two-year running of the statute of limitations; thus, the patient lost the right to sue and the case was dismissed. Even though the EMT was negligent, the patient was prevented from recovering damages.

The time limits set by statutes of limitation vary throughout the United States. For example, some states require that negligence claims be brought within two years of the date of negligent treatment; others require that such claims be brought within three years. Additionally, some states may allow these time limits to be extended under certain circumstances. For example, a statute of limitation that requires that a negligence claim be brought within two years may permit an extension from the date the patient reasonably discovered that the treatment rendered was negligent (instead of the actual date of negligent treatment).

The statute of limitation defense, when applicable, is a complete defense—a patient can be barred entirely from pursuing a negligence claim if the EMT was negligent in rendering prehospital care and the negligence resulted in injury to the patient. EMTs should consult their supervisors or local attorneys to determine the applicable statutes of limitation in their states.

3.5.4 Comparative/Contributory Negligence

Many states have *comparative/contributory negligence laws*, which provide that damages that the plaintiff may be allowed to recover are reduced in proportion to the plaintiff's percentage of negligence. The specifics of these laws vary from state to state. Generally, however, the plaintiff can only recover damages if the fault attributed to the plaintiff is less than that attributed to the defendant. Consider Field Incident Example 3-19.

Field Incident Example 3-19

Facts. An EMT is called to the scene of a fall involving a patient with a suspected neck injury. The patient is alert and oriented but opposes the EMT's attempts at neck immobilization. If the EMT persisted in the attempts, the patient might be convinced to allow neck stabilization. However, the EMT merely tells the patient to climb into the ambulance. Upon arrival at the hospital, the patient is found to be permanently paralyzed from a cervical spine injury. Proper neck immobilization would have prevented this injury.

Question. Can the patient recover 100 percent of the damages because the EMT negligently failed to insist on neck immobilization?

Analysis. If this state has a comparative negligence law, it is likely the patient will only be permitted to recover damages in proportion to the fault of the respective parties. In this situation, a jury would likely find the EMT negligent, but also would likely find the patient comparatively negligent and the damages would be reduced accordingly. If the jury found that the patient's negligence was greater than the EMT's, the patient generally would not be allowed to collect any damages.

Comparative negligence laws sometimes act as a partial defense to a negligence claim. As long as the patient's negligence is less than the EMT's, the patient may be allowed to collect some but not all damages sustained as a result of the EMT's negligence. If the patient's negligence is greater than the EMT's, the comparative negligence law may act as a complete defense and the patient may not be permitted to collect any damages even though the EMT was negligent to some degree.

3.5.5 Governmental Immunity

The defense of *governmental immunity* applies only to an EMT who is employed by a governmental unit, such as a municipal fire department or county hospital. Individuals employed by private pre-hospital care providers do not benefit from this defense.

Historically, federal, state, and local governments could not be sued without the government's consent. Therefore, unless a government expressly allowed itself to be sued, even meritorious claims could not be brought. Most governmental units now permit lawsuits, but with certain limitations and restrictions. Laws that describe the circumstances under which a governmental unit may be sued are *tort claims acts*.

Tort claims acts may require that before a lawsuit is filed, notice be given to the governmental unit within a certain time after the incident that may lead to a claim. Failure to give this notice usually results in dismissal of the plaintiff's claim. The time within which the notice must be given acts as a form of statute of limitations. If notice is not given within the required time, then the plaintiff is thereafter prohibited from bringing any claim, even if meritorious, against the governmental unit.

In many states, tort claims acts contain limits on the amount of damages a plaintiff may collect. For example, a tort claims law may set a cap on the total amount of money a plaintiff can recover from a single incident. If a jury awards damages in excess of this tort claims limit, the plaintiff cannot collect the excess amount.

Some states, however, have relinquished their right to immunity with no conditions or restrictions. In such states, governmental units may be sued like any private person or entity.

Tort claims acts can offer a complete or partial defense to a negligence claim. If the plaintiff fails to give proper notice or fails to bring the claim within the required time limit, tort claims acts offer a complete defense because the plaintiff's claim will be dismissed. If the plaintiff is allowed to recover damages but those damages are capped, tort claims acts offer a partial defense.

3.6 DEFENSES TO NEGLIGENCE: CONCLUSIONS

A plaintiff who has an otherwise valid claim of negligence against an EMT may be prevented or limited in the recovery of damages because of certain defenses to negligence. Good Samaritan laws, immunity statutes, statutes of limitation, and governmental immunity laws may prevent a plaintiff from obtaining any damages at all. Comparative/contributory negligence and governmental immunity laws may reduce the amount of damages the plaintiff is allowed to recover. However, the specifics of these defenses differ from state to state; therefore, each EMT should consult his or her local attorney or supervisor on specific questions about the state laws.

NOTES

1. U.S. Department of Transportation, National Highway Traffic Safety Administration. *Emergency Medical Services Dispatcher: National Standard Curriculum.* Washington, D.C.: U.S. Government Printing Office, 1983.

2. *Principles of Emergency Medical Dispatch,* Jeff Clawson and Kate Dernocour, Prentice-Hall, 1988.

3. Vt. Stat. Ann. tit. 12, § 519(a) (1972 & Supp. 1982).

4. Minn. Stat. Ann. § 604.05(1) (West 1984).

5. Mont. Code Ann. § 61-8-107 (1987).

6. Cal. Health & Safety Code, Div. 2.5, § 1799.102 (West 1986).

7. Mass. Gen. L. ch. 111C, § 14 (1977).

8. Texas Civ. Stat. art. 4447o, §3.18 (1985).

9. Cal. Health & Safety Code Div. 2.5, § 1799.106 (West 1988).

Chapter 4

Standard of Care

4.1 STANDARD OF CARE: DUTY TO PROVIDE QUALITY CARE

As discussed in 3.2.1 on negligence, the law imposes an obligation or duty on emergency medical technicians (EMTs) to conform with medically recognized standards of care, a term that is synonymous with duty within the concept of negligence. EMTs who violate the standard of care breach their duty of care toward a patient. In this chapter, the standard of care and its application to claims of EMT negligence are explored.

4.2 STANDARD OF CARE

Within the element of duty, a plaintiff must show that an EMT failed to adhere to the standard of care under particular circumstances. If a violation of the standard of care is proven, the plaintiff also proves a breach of duty toward the particular patient. To carry the burden of proof on this critical element of negligence, the plaintiff must establish the standard of care and how it was violated. However, note that the standard of care measured is that standard governing at the time of the incident, not at the time the lawsuit is filed.

***

Field Incident Example 4-1

Facts. An EMT responding to an emergency call using lights and siren travels through an intersection against a red light at a speed of sixty-three miles per hour. A collision ensues, resulting in the death of the driver of the car broadsided by the ambulance.

Questions. What did the standard of care require of this ambulance driver who approached and traveled through the controlled intersection? How is the EMT's duty measured in relation to the established standard of care?

Analysis. In all EMS systems, the standard of care for this situation requires that an EMT drive with due regard for the safety of others. That is, the EMT's duty is to drive carefully so that passengers in the ambulance or others are not injured. The standard of care acts as a measure of the EMT's conduct. If the EMT's actions do not meet or do not exceed the requisite standard of care, the EMT then breaches his or her duty toward the patient. In this example, it is fair to say that driving through an intersection at sixty-three miles per hour, with or without lights and siren, violates the established standard of care. This EMT's conduct, measured against the prescribed standard of care, thus represents a breach of duty toward all drivers, but particularly the driver of the car struck by the ambulance.

***

The standard of care must be evaluated in any prehospital care incident before further examination is justified. Five sources establish the standard of care:

1. state statutes and administrative rules
2. local ordinances and codes
3. written and verbal treatment protocols
4. medical textbooks and journal articles
5. physician directors and expert witnesses

An EMT must rely on these sources to understand the standard of care in the community. Similarly, the plaintiff must rely on these sources to prove that the standard of care was violated in a particular case.

4.2.1 State Statutes and Administrative Rules

The primary source of any standard of care are state statutes and administrative rules. These laws set forth the state's education, training, and certification requirements for an EMT. An EMT must comply with these laws to become and remain certified. For example, TEX. ADMIN. CODE §157.76 (1984) requires continuing education for recertification. An EMT who is found to be practicing with an invalid certificate may be in violation of the standard of care. Although it may be difficult for a plaintiff to prove that lack of certification directly resulted in injury to the patient, evidence that an EMT failed to comply with the state recertification law may lead to a presumption that the EMT was unqualified to perform the procedures being examined in the particular case.

State statutes and administrative rules set forth the EMT's *scope of practice*, or the outermost boundary of the EMT's authority. For example, Cal. Health & Safety Code, §1997.171 (West, 1988) and accompanying Administrative Rules set forth the scope of practice for intermediate level EMTs. It lists in detail those procedures a certified EMT-II may perform at the scene of a medical emergency or during transport. An EMT who performs treatment procedures not included in this scope of practice will be presumed to have acted outside the standard of care.

EMTs must be familiar with state statutes and administrative rules so that the EMTs may conform to all standards of care. EMTs may obtain copies of these laws from their states' emergency medical services (EMS) agency. In a negligence lawsuit, the plaintiff's lawyer will examine these laws in detail to determine if the EMT met all statutory requirements. Failure to comply with the criteria of state laws or having acted outside stated boundaries may be evidence of a violation of the standard of care.

4.2.2 Local Ordinances and Codes

Local ordinances and codes provide another source of the standard of care. Like state laws and administrative rules, local ordinances and codes set forth requirements that an EMT must follow. Although not all cities, counties, or special service districts have ordinances or codes, an EMT must comply with the requirements of such laws where they do exist.

Local laws work in conjunction with state laws to create standards applicable to a particular EMS system. Generally, local laws must provide standards at least equal to those set by the state. However, local laws may set more stringent standards. For example, local laws may require more hours of continuing education and training than state law. Local laws, though, cannot set less stringent standards. For example, if state law prohibits EMTs from performing a particular medical procedure, a local system or EMS provider by local rule cannot supersede this limited scope of practice and allow local EMTs to perform procedures prohibited by state law.

In any case involving a prehospital care provider, the plaintiff's lawyer will check local law, as well as state law, to establish the regulatory framework within which the EMT functions. The EMT's actual conduct then will be evaluated in comparison with this regulatory structure. EMT actions outside of this legal framework are evidence that the EMT violated the standard of care.

4.2.3 Written and Verbal Treatment Protocols

Local treatment protocols constitute perhaps the most important element of the standard of care. Because local treatment protocols generally are developed in conformance with state and local law with input from the local and national medical community, these protocols provide the basis for the standard of care in many prehospital care systems. The plaintiff in a negligence lawsuit will compare carefully the treatment rendered by an EMT with the requirements of local treatment protocols. Any deviation from these protocols is evidence of a violation of the standard of care. The EMT's best defense is to conscientiously follow local treatment protocols.

Written protocols have been adopted by many EMS systems and providers throughout the United States. Other systems use such verbal protocols as on-line medical control for on-scene medical direction. In such systems, physicians or specially trained nurses provide treatment direction by radio or telephone. In any EMS system, written treatment protocols constitute a better quality assurance mechanism than verbal orders because written orders in the form of protocols provide EMTs with specific guidelines to follow in particular situations. An EMT who has a written document to study and memorize is in a better position to meet the standard of care than an EMT who constantly has to rely on radio or telephone advice. In contrast, verbal orders via radio or telephone may vary depending on the situation. Verbal, on-line advice should be used to supplement written treatment protocols to assure standard of care compliance.

4.2.4 Medical Textbooks and Journal Articles

In a case involving a prehospital care provider, the plaintiff's lawyer, in evaluating the standard of care, will compare the EMT's conduct with medical textbooks and journal articles in which appropriate treatment in similar prehospital care situations is discussed. If the medical literature offers recommendations for different treatment than what the EMT provided, then the EMT may be found to have violated the standard of care. Note, though, that the medical literature is intended to supplement, not replace, local treatment protocols. For example, if protocols require the use of pneumatic antishock trousers under certain circumstances and a medical journal article suggests that such a device should not be used, the article does not override the local protocol. However, should the local medical community change the protocol based on the literature, the EMT must follow the new protocol and cease using antishock trousers. On the other hand, local protocols may advise neck and back immobilization in cases involving suspected neck injury and medical textbooks and journal articles may provide reliable advice on how spine immobilization is best accomplished. The knowledge of and failure to follow this reliable advice may constitute a violation of the standard of care.

It is important that EMTs subscribe to and read relevant prehospital care journals to keep abreast of the new developments in prehospital care. Furthermore, EMTs have a duty to know changes in the standard of care because the EMTs will be held accountable for this knowledge in the legal setting. Because the best defense is a good offense, an EMT who keeps abreast of developments in prehospital care by regularly reading current literature is less likely to commit a standard of care violation.

4.2.5 Physician Directors and Expert Witnesses

In the prehospital care setting, physician directors are or should be involved directly in the development of local prehospital care protocols to establish the standard of care. In the legal setting, expert witnesses interpret these protocols and apply protocol requirements to the facts of a particular case to determine whether the standard of care has been met.

Many EMS systems, especially those in which advanced life support (ALS) equipment and personnel are used, employ physician directors in all areas of protocol development and quality assurance. Many state laws require that ALS systems have a physician director as a condition to providing ALS care. For example, CAL. HEALTH & SAFETY CODE § 1797.202 (West 1986) provides that

> Every local EMS agency shall have a full or part time licensed physician and surgeon as medical director . . . to provide medical control and to assure medical accountability throughout the planning, implementation and evaluation of the EMS system.

State laws such as this one envision physician involvement in all phases of the EMS system. From a standard of care perspective, the physician should have an active involvement in protocol development, evaluation of standard of care compliance, and continuing education. The greater the involvement of the physician director, the clearer the standard of care in a particular system because the standards set in a system will be defined and articulated more clearly and, therefore, communicated to and understood more easily by EMTs in the system. The importance of the physician director in protocol development and standard of care compliance cannot be overemphasized.

Before and during the litigation process, the plaintiff's lawyer will retain expert witnesses to evaluate the facts of the case in light of the EMS system's standard of care. The experts will view the EMT's conduct in the context of state and local laws, local protocols, and textbook and journal articles. They will consult physicians experienced in prehospital care as well as EMTs or paramedics familiar with the particular system's standards of care. These experts, as well as those hired by the defense lawyer once litigation has begun, will compare the EMT's actions with medically recognized standards to determine whether the EMT conformed to the standard of care.

4.3 CONCLUSIONS

The standard of care represents a measure against which the EMT's actions will be compared. This measure is derived from state and local laws, local treatment protocols, medical textbooks and journal articles, and health care professionals experienced in prehospital care.

The standard of care evolves. In litigation, the standard of care that is established and evaluated is the standard that existed at the time of the incident, not the standard of care in existence at the time of trial. For example, the use of sandbags for neck stabilization has been a common and accepted practice for a long time. Current literature suggests that the use of sandbags may be detrimental to the patient. Based on this literature, some EMS systems have changed their neck stabilization protocols by replacing sandbags with other, more acceptable, stabilization devices. If an EMT is sued for failing to properly immobilize a patient's neck, the protocol in effect at the time of the call controls. If a situation called for the use of sandbags and the former protocol required the use of sandbags, but the EMT failed to use sandbags, he or she has violated the standard of care notwithstanding the fact that the protocol *now* prohibits sandbag use.

The standard of care also has evolved in trauma system development. Since the early days of prehospital care, general standards of care have required that an ambulance transport an emergency patient to the nearest hospital. With the advent of trauma systems, this standard is changing. In many formalized trauma systems, certain hospitals are bypassed so the patient is transported not to the closest hospital, but to the closest *trauma* hospital.[1] Medical research has shown that patients who meet certain criteria would benefit from treatment at a definitive care facility even if the facility were located farther away.[2]

Proving a violation of the standard of care is the same as proving a breach of duty. The best protection for the EMT against a negligence claim is a thorough awareness and understanding of the laws and protocols in effect in the particular EMS system as well as a thorough awareness of all current medical literature. By gaining such an awareness, an EMT can become well versed on the applicable standard of care. Although adherence to the standard of care does not guarantee that an EMT will be immune from a claim of negligence, it does provide the best defense to such a claim. An EMT who conforms to the requisite standard of care has not breached a duty toward the patient; therefore, no liability follows.

NOTES

1. *See, for example,* Or. Rev. Stat. § 431.607 (1987) et seq.

2. *See, for example,* Pepe, Paul E. et al, The Relationship Between Total Prehospital Time and Outcome in Hypotensive Victims of Penetrating Injuries, *Annals of Emergency Medicine*, Vol. 16, March 1987, p. 293 and Cales, Richard H., Trauma Mortality in Orange County: The Effect of Implementation of a Regional Trauma System, *Annals of Emergency Medicine*, Vol. 13, January 1984, p. 1.

Chapter **5**

Consent and Refusal

5.1 CONSENT AND REFUSAL

One recurring issue facing prehospital care providers involves problems of consent and refusal. The question of patient acquiescence to medical treatment and transport is of critical importance to an emergency medical technician (EMT). In this chapter, the complex concepts of consent and refusal in the prehospital care setting are explored. Additionally, requirements for valid consent, including legal and mental capacity, means of consent, scope of consent, and issues of patient refusal are discussed.

5.1.1 Consent

Consent is a voluntary agreement by a patient who is both legally and mentally capable of making decisions regarding treatment or transport. A patient must be able to understand the circumstances of an illness or injury and make a choice based on that understanding. Coercion, intimidation, or force do not result in voluntary agreement.

At the heart of the consent process is a choice to accept or reject treatment. Consent requires that the patient provide information to the EMT so that the EMT can provide information to the patient. Following this exchange of information, the patient agrees to or refuses treatment. The EMT must remember that the patient decides whether to allow or to refuse medical care.

5.1.2 Treatment without Consent

An EMT should understand that all qualified individuals, with some exceptions, have a right to decide what medical intervention, if any, is permissible. This absolute privilege for an individual to control his or her own fate is central to the notion of the right to self-determination. Health care providers cannot treat patients who do not wish to be treated. An EMT who treats a patient without consent may face liability. A patient treated without consent may sue the EMT under at least three legal theories: (1) medical assault and battery, (2) false imprisonment, and (3) negligent consent.

Civil assault involves placing a patient in fear of being touched without consent. Civil battery is the actual touching of the patient without consent. In a successful lawsuit, a patient must show that the EMT examined, treated, or transported without express or implied consent. The EMT who takes the blood pressure of or applies a dressing to a competent patient who specifically refuses any type of treatment may be liable for medical assault and battery regardless of the patient's need for medical treatment.

The legal theory of false imprisonment is the intentional confinement of a person without that person's consent and without some lawful reason for the confinement. A competent, nonconsenting patient may bring such a lawsuit if, for example, an EMT transports the patient without permission to a facility other than the one specifically requested. This potential theory of liability raises interesting questions in the prehospital care context. Consider Field Incident Example 5-1 and Case Summary 5-1.

Field Incident Example 5-1

Facts. EMTs are treating a patient complaining of chest pain who is in need of transport to a hospital. The patient is located in a rural community with only one hospital located three miles away. The patient's physician is on staff at a city hospital located twenty-five miles away. The patient will only consent to transport to the distant city hospital and the patient is stable enough for transport this distance. The EMTs are staffing the community's only ambulance, and transport to the distant hospital would deprive the community of emergency ambulance service for approximately two hours.

Questions. Must the EMTs transport the patient to the distant city hospital? Does transport to the local hospital against the patient's wishes constitute false imprisonment?

Analysis. Transport to a hospital other than the one chosen by the patient technically constitutes false imprisonment because the patient is being confined within the ambulance and transported to another location without the patient's consent. The fact that the community's only ambulance will be out of service locally for two hours does not justify falsely imprisoning the patient. The EMS crew should discuss this problem with the patient and attempt to get consent to transport to the local hospital. Perhaps arrangements could be made to transport first to the local hospital with immediate arrangements to then transfer the patient to the hospital of choice. The patient may consent to local transport if such arrangements are possible. Without such consent, the EMTs may be liable for false imprisonment if they should transport the patient to the local hospital.

Case Summary 5-1

Case Citation. Wideman v. Shallowford Community Hospital, Inc., 826 F.2d 1030 (Georgia 11th Cir. 1987).

Facts. The plaintiff, Ms. Wideman, was four months pregnant and began experiencing abdominal pains. She called her obstetrician who instructed her to come immediately to Piedmont Hospital where he would meet her. Ms. Wideman called the county's 911 emergency telephone number and requested that an ambulance take her to Piedmont Hospital. According to the plaintiff, a unit from the county's emergency medical services (EMS) agency responded. Request was made for transport to Piedmont, but the EMTs refused and insisted on transporting Ms. Wideman to Shallowford Comunity Hospital. As a result of the delay in receiving obstetrical care,

Ms. Wideman gave birth to a premature baby who died four hours after birth.

The Widemans sued Shallowford Hospital, the county, and the three EMS employees who staffed the responding unit. The Widemans claimed deprivation of certain federal constitutional rights and state claims of false imprisonment, negligence, and intentional infliction of emotional distress.

Analysis. The court held that the Widemans were not deprived of any constitutionally protected rights. However, the court indicated that if the plaintiff were able to prove the alleged facts, the plaintiff might have meritorious state claims, including a claim for false imprisonment.

This case highlights the liability risk faced by a prehospital care provider who transports a patient to a location other than that requested by the patient. A false imprisonment claim may follow such an action.

Another legal theory on which a patient can base a lawsuit, the negligence theory of consent, arises when the patient suffers an injury as a result of consent to a certain form of medical treatment. The patient claims that the health care provider failed to disclose certain information, the disclosure of which would have affected the patient's decision regarding treatment. In essence, the patient claims that, with proper disclosure, treatment would have been refused and the injury avoided. This claim usually arises in the physician–patient context; no cases in which this theory has been applied to the prehospital care setting exist.

5.2 REQUIREMENTS FOR VALID CONSENT OR REFUSAL

For a patient to give and the EMT to receive valid consent, the patient must possess *both* legal and mental capacity or power.

5.2.1 Legal Capacity

Capacity in legal terms simply means legally qualified. In the context of consent, legal capacity means legally qualified to give consent.

Generally, every person is presumed to be qualified to give consent, that is, to possess legal capacity. As with every general rule, exceptions exist. These exceptions are discussed in 5.2.1.1, 5.2.1.2, and 5.2.1.3.

5.2.1.1 Guardianships

When a person is unable to care for himself or herself, a court may appoint a *guardian* for that person. A guardian is a person who is invested lawfully with the power of managing another person's affairs because that person cannot do so. A guardian may be appointed to an adult or to a minor (a person who has not obtained the age of majority, generally age 18, or who is younger than the age of legal competence).

Once a guardian is appointed by a court to manage a person's affairs, that person becomes a ward of the court. The ward does not have legal capacity. In the medical context, this means that a ward of the court cannot give valid consent for treatment or transport. Instead, only the guardian can consent to or refuse medical intervention on behalf of the ward/patient, whether the patient is an adult or a minor.

An EMT who must treat a patient under a guardianship may be confronted with the dilemma of who should give consent to treatment. If both the guardian and the patient desire medical intervention, clearly the EMT may initiate treatment and transport the patient. If the patient is an adult who attempts to refuse treatment despite the guardian's consent, the situation becomes more complex. However, once a guardian is appointed, the patient loses legal capacity to consent to or to refuse treatment. If the guardian authorizes treatment, then the EMT may proceed despite the patient's refusal.

It is important that the EMT demand proof that the person who claims to be the guardian actually has legal authority to act on the patient's behalf. Proof may include a court order or other legal document. Additionally, the EMS provider's attorney should review applicable state law to determine the authority that may be vested in a guardian for purposes of managing a patient's medical care.

5.2.1.2 Prisoners and Arrestees

Generally, incarceration or detention does not deny an individual the right to make decisions regarding medical treatment. However, some states have enacted laws that affect prisoner rights to determine treatment. EMTs often must treat prisoners and individuals under arrest; thus, this section focuses on the laws that affect the consent and refusal rights of individuals in custody.

Because people who lack legal capacity, such as prisoners in some states, cannot give valid consent, some states authorize administrative officers of correctional facilities to give consent instead. The scope of consent in prisons varies from state to state. EMTs with EMS providers that receive calls to treat prisoners should check local law to determine the scope of consent and the requirements necessary to obtain third-party consent on behalf of a prisoner.

One legal principle, which allows treatment without express consent and applies to prisoners and arrestees, is the *emergency doctrine*. In prisons, the emergency doctrine states that treatment may be provided by the health practitioner if the person in custody is in need of lifesaving care and if the individual is incapable of giving consent as a result of injuries or another health condition. If *both* of these conditions are present, an EMT may treat and transport even without the prisoner's express consent. However, if the prisoner is capable of and does, in fact, refuse treatment, further medical intervention is prohibited unless someone else is authorized to consent on the individual's behalf.

One perplexing problem facing many EMTs involves the level of cooperation with law enforcement officers that is appropriate in the field. Consider Field Incident Example 5-2.

Field Incident Example 5-2

Facts. An EMS unit is called to the scene of an automobile accident. Police officers are on the scene and suspect that the injured driver of one vehicle is under the influence of alcohol. The officer asks the EMT treating this individual to draw a blood sample for later criminal analysis. Local protocols do not require or authorize the EMT to draw a blood sample in this situation, given the patient's history and medical condition.

Question. Should the EMT draw the blood sample at the officer's request?

Analysis. At the outset, it should be made clear the EMT's duty is to the patient and not to the police officer. EMTs are not law enforcement investigators and have only limited authority to take part in evidence gathering. Except for a state law or a court order to the contrary, the EMT should not draw blood or perform any other unnecessary medical procedure at the request of a law enforcement officer. The EMT who performs unnecessary medical procedures without *proper* authority may face liability.

An otherwise competent individual does not lose the legal capacity to consent or refuse treatment simply because he or she is suspected of breaking the law. In some states, blood samples are authorized by certain health care providers when the patient is unconscious or otherwise incapacitated. EMTs should check to see if any such laws apply to the EMT's locality and should investigate the scope of these laws.

Generally, rules of consent and refusal do not vary simply because a person is in custody. In dealing with a prisoner or an arrestee, EMTs must remember that the individual possesses the legal capacity to consent to or to refuse medical treatment or transportation. Unless state law deprives the person of this right, the individual's wishes must govern.

5.2.1.3 Minors

The third class of individuals affected by the concept of legal capacity is minors. EMTs frequently encounter ill or injured minors. A situation in which a parent is not available to expressly authorize treatment of a minor can be quite frustrating to an EMT who wishes to care for the youth.

Under the traditional legal rule, a minor cannot give consent for treatment because minors do not possess the legal capacity or qualification to grant consent. Because minors are legally incapable of giving consent, an EMT must obtain consent from the minor's parent or other person authorized to consent on behalf of the minor.

The Emergency Exception. The general rule that minors cannot determine the course of their own medical treatment has exceptions. The first and most important of these exceptions involves treatment of minors in emergency situations. The exception says that if a minor requires immediate lifesaving treatment or care to prevent serious injury, an EMT can treat and transport without consent.

The term "emergency" is likely to be defined broadly by the courts and the exception discussed in terms of implied consent by the parents. In other words, the courts may suggest that the parents would have consented to treatment if they knew of the child's situation. Some states have statutes that authorize treatment of minors in certain emergency situations without consent from a parent or guardian. However, an EMT involved in a lawsuit by a parent or guardian for the unconsented treatment of a minor child carries the burden of showing the nature of the emergency and the reason the child required immediate treatment. An EMT should not consider the emergency exception as a license to treat all minors without consent, regardless of circumstances.

If an EMT treats a minor in a nonemergency situation without the consent of a person who is authorized to consent on the minor's behalf, liability may follow. Successful lawsuits for civil battery have been brought against physicians who treated minors without parental consent. Such an action also may be brought against an EMT successfully. A lawsuit involving an EMT most likely would be combined with a claim for injury or death if the EMT treated without consent in a nonemergency situation and if the EMT's negligence resulted in injury to a child. The child's parent in such a situation could sue the EMT for negligence and battery.

Mature and Emancipated Minors. Some states give certain minors the right to consent to their own treatment. These laws generally address two classes of minors: (1) mature minors and (2) emancipated minors.

Mature minors, despite their chronological age, are recognized as being able to give informed consent, or as possessing legal capacity, because of their ability to understand and appreciate the nature and consequences of treatment or nontreatment. Before determining whether a minor is mature for purposes of consent, the courts will examine the circumstances of the minor's age, intelligence, and ability to understand the nature of the medical emergency. Because an EMT's determination of what constitutes a mature minor may differ from that of a court, an EMT should not rely on this exception.

In some states, emancipated minors also are given the right to consent to their own treatment. A minor may be declared legally emancipated for limited purposes. Once a minor is legally emancipated, he or she may be treated as an adult, who possesses legal capacity, in specific circumstances. The courts consider several factors to determine if a minor is emancipated. These factors include whether the minor is living independently, is self-supporting, married, or in the armed services. The presence of any or all of these factors may influence a court's decision about the capability of a minor to give consent to treatment. Again, an EMT should not rely on this exception unless the minor possesses a legal document granting the right to give consent.

State Laws Affecting the Treatment of Minors. Some states grant certain groups of minors legal capacity to give consent to medical treatment. Generally, these laws set a minimum age at which a minor can consent, the kinds of medical treatment to which a minor can consent, and criteria that must be met before a minor is authorized to consent. An Oregon law, for example, provides that

> a minor 15 years of age or older, may give consent to hospital care, medical or surgical diagnosis or treatment by a physician licensed by the Board of Medical Examiners for the State of Oregon . . . without the consent of a parent or guardian. . . .[1]

Note that the Oregon law does not allow this class of minors to consent to prehospital care rendered by an EMT. Other states have similar laws. An EMT should check state law to determine whether statutes exist that affect a minor's right to give consent and how these laws apply in the prehospital care setting.

Some statutes grant immunity from liability for unauthorized care of minors. Although requirements vary, these statutes generally require that, to receive immunity for unauthorized treatment, an EMT possess the good faith belief that a minor was authorized to give consent under the terms of a statute granting minors legal capacity. For example, a Utah law provides that

> no certified basic or advanced life support personnel shall be subject to civil liability for failure to obtain consent in rendering emergency medical care authorized by this chapter to any individual regardless of age who is unable to give his consent where there is no other person present legally authorized to consent to emergency treatment, provided that such personnel act in good faith. . . .[2]

To be shielded from civil liability under the Utah law, an EMT must render emergency medical care in good faith. This immunity, however, does not protect an EMT from liability for acts of negligence. Thus, treatment of the minor must be in accordance with the community's standard of care. An EMT should check state law to determine if his or her state has a similar law.

An EMT who treats a minor authorized to give consent often must consider whether he or she should inform a minor's parents about the patient's condition, treatment, and location. Many states have passed parental disclosure laws that vary in their approach to this controversial subject. Generally, though, states authorize certain health care professionals, primarily physicians, to disclose information about the minor patient to the parents only under specified conditions. For example, one state forbids disclosure unless the physician feels notification is essential to the minor's life or health. Another state, Oregon, provides blanket immunity to physicians, hospitals, and dentists if disclosure is made to a parent under certain specified conditions.[3] Before an EMT discloses information about a minor to the legally competent minor patient's parents, the EMT should consult state law to learn about the conditions that are required before disclosure can occur.

Refusal by or on Behalf of a Minor. Occasionally, EMTs encounter a parent who refuses treatment of his or her minor child. The parent's refusal may place the child in jeopardy as well as place an EMT in an awkward position. Although the courts will intervene to consent on behalf of the seriously ill child if the minor's condition is life- or health-threatening, in the field setting, there is little time to obtain a court order authorizing treatment. Thus, an EMT is faced with two choices: (1) treat the child despite the parent's refusal or (2) do not treat the child according to the parent's wishes.

In the situation involving parental refusal of treatment for a seriously ill or injured child, an EMT should contact immediately medical control for on-line medical advice. The on-line medical control physician can speak directly with the parent to persuade the parent to consent for the child. If medical control is unavailable or attempts at persuasion are unsuccessful, a law enforcement officer can be called to the scene. In many areas, a law enforcement officer can place the child in temporary protective custody and authorize treatment on the child's behalf.

In the field setting where neither medical control nor law enforcement are available, the EMT is faced with a difficult choice. Practically speaking, the only course of action the EMT can take is to treat the child despite the parent's desires. However, such action may result in a lawsuit for unauthorized treatment, including theories of medical assault and battery or false imprisonment. Yet, if the EMT does not treat the child because of parental refusal, the EMT still may be subject to a lawsuit for wrongful death or serious injury. The parents, after observing the tragic results of their refusal, may deny their refusal and sue the EMT for abandonment. A jury that hears a case involving a now healthy child who was treated despite parental refusal is less likely to award substantial damages than a jury that determines fault for abandonment of the same child. Generally, an EMT is better off erring conservatively and treating the child.

An EMT who encounters parental refusal involving a child who is not seriously ill or injured must seek and obtain a court order before treating the child. Courts are less likely to authorize medical intervention in such situations because they recognize the parent's right to consent to or refuse treatment on behalf of the child. In nonemergency circumstances, the EMT must respect the parent's choice.

Treatment of Minors: Conclusions. EMTs, who regularly face ill or injured minors in the course of their work, must presume that the minors are legally incapable of giving consent. If no state law authorizing a minor to give consent exists, an EMT may treat a minor without consent only in an emergency. In nonemergency situations, however, treatment cannot be rendered without the consent of someone authorized to consent on the minor's behalf. If a parent refuses treatment, then, generally, the EMT cannot treat. Whether treatment should be rendered despite parental refusal depends on the circumstances of the particular case and the resources available. The EMT who understands when consent is required and who may give consent will significantly reduce his or her chances of being sued by a distraught parent or guardian for the nonconsensual treatment of a child.

5.2.2 Mental Capacity

Mental capacity is another requirement for valid consent or refusal. Mental capacity, or competence, relates to a person's state of mind. The law presumes that a person possesses the requisite mental capacity to reach an informed choice about and to understand the nature and consequences of authorizing treatment or transport. Every competent person has the absolute right to consent to or to refuse medical intervention.

An incompetent person, one who lacks mental capacity, by law cannot give valid consent or refusal because, for any number of reasons, he or she cannot understand why treatment is necessary or what risks he or she faces by refusing treatment.

A person's ability to understand the nature and consequences of accepting or rejecting treatment can be affected by mental illness, serious injury or illness, drugs, or alcohol. An EMT must consider these factors when evaluating a person's mental capacity, or competence, to consent to or to refuse medical intervention.

Field Incident Example 5-3

Facts. An EMT unit responds to the scene of an automobile accident. A car struck a tree injuring the sole occupant, the driver. Following a brief physical examination by the EMT, the patient states he does not want further medical intervention or transportation to the hospital. The EMT notes odor of alcohol on the patient's breath; bloodshot eyes; slightly slurred speech; disorientation to time, place, and person; laceration over the right eyebrow; and a bruise on the left arm.

Question. Is this patient competent to refuse medical care?

Analysis. In this case, factors affecting the patient's competence include the possibilities of intoxication and head injury from the accident. To determine the patient's mental capacity, the EMT must do a more thorough evaluation of the patient's condition, assess the effects of the alcohol, and determine the extent of the head injury. As in all cases, it is important for the EMT to document all symptoms, actions, and events on a prehospital care report form.

After objectively evaluating a patient's ability to make an informed choice regarding acceptance or refusal of prehospital care, an EMT will determine the patient's competency. If the patient is competent, the EMT is free to treat with consent or rely on valid refusal without fear of liability consequences. If the patient is incompetent, the situation is more complex because an incompetent patient cannot give valid consent or refusal. How the EMT is to proceed depends on the seriousness of the patient's condition.

The EMT who encounters an incompetent patient who is not experiencing a life- or health-threatening emergency cannot treat without the consent of someone authorized to consent on the patient's behalf because the patient is mentally incapable of giving valid consent. For example, some state laws authorize a parent to give consent for a mentally incapacitated adult child. In other states, a court order authorizing treatment for a mentally incapacitated adult must be obtained. If no emergency exists, the EMT is not authorized to initiate treatment and should contact medical control for advice.

Consent, however, is unnecessary if an emergency exists. For the EMT, this is perhaps the most important exception to the rule prohibiting treatment without consent. For an EMT to treat a patient without consent, two factors *must* be present. First, the patient must be unable to exercise the mental ability to make an informed decision about treatment as a result of a severe incapacity. This means the person must be unable to understand the facts, risks, and alternatives of accepting or rejecting treatment or transportation because of his or her medical condition. Second, a true emergency must exist. The patient must be suffering from a life- or health-threatening illness or injury that requires immediate treatment. Although the emergency exception is viewed as treatment without consent, it constitutes a form of implied consent.

An EMT must be able to document the patient's mental incapacity and the seriousness of the patient's condition, although the courts likely will interpret these findings broadly. The emergency exception should not be viewed as a means of treating every patient under the influence of drugs or alcohol or every victim of serious trauma. Mental incapacity in conjunction with life- or health-threatening illness or injury must exist or the EMT will risk liability for unauthorized treatment. One of the most difficult situations an EMT faces is that involving a patient who is intermittently lucid. Consider Field Incident Example 5-4.

Field Incident Example 5-4

Facts. An advanced life support unit responds to a call involving an unconscious diabetic patient. Because the patient is incapable of giving consent because of mental incapacity (unconsciousness) and an emergency exists, the EMTs treat in accordance with the emergency exception and local protocols. Following the infusion of intravenous glucose, the patient awakens and refuses further treatment.

Question. Should the EMTs proceed with treatment of this patient or respect his or her wishes to discontinue intervention?

Analysis. First, the EMTs must determine whether the patient is competent. If, after careful evaluation, they conclude that the patient indeed does understand the nature and circumstances of refusing treatment and transport, the EMTs must comply with the patient's wishes and discontinue treatment. If, however, the EMTs conclude that the patient is incompetent and therefore incapable of consenting to or refusing treatment, they must determine if an emergency exists. If the patient is incompetent and an emergency exists, then treatment may commence. If an emergency does not exist, then treatment cannot proceed without consent from someone authorized to consent on the patient's behalf.

An important consideration regarding the patient in this case is the possibility that the patient may lose consciousness again after the EMTs depart the scene. Although this risk exists and has been explained in detail to the patient, the EMT must recognize that the patient, if competent, has the right to refuse even lifesaving intervention. Until the patient again becomes unconscious, treatment may not be continued.

Situations involving determinations of competence coupled with the seriousness of the patient's condition force an EMT to make decisions quickly about whether and how to proceed. Care must be taken in such situations to avoid liability. The competent patient has a right to consent to or refuse medical intervention. The incompetent patient requires intervention to avoid liability. Thus, it is essential that an EMT carefully assess the patient's ability to understand the nature and consequences of accepting or refusing treatment.

5.3 MEANS OF CONSENT

Consent may be given in writing, orally, or by conduct. Rarely, if ever, will an EMT obtain written consent for treatment. Consent normally will be obtained either verbally or through the conduct of the patient.

Consent is categorized as either express or implied. Express consent exists when a patient affirmatively tells the EMT to proceed with treatment. Thus, if a patient verbally conveys a desire to be treated by the EMT, express consent has been granted. Implied consent arises from the patient's conduct under certain circumstances. Thus, if a patient is silent and capable of objecting when treatment is initiated, consent is implied. Similarly, if the patient nods affirmatively when asked by the EMT whether treatment may begin or by other actions manifests a desire for treatment to begin or continue, consent is implied. Implied consent also arises in an emergency. For example, if an EMT encounters an unconscious person, the law presumes that the person would consent if able.

Exercise 5-1

Facts. An EMS unit responds to a call involving a building collapse. Three patients are injured. As an EMT approaches, patient 1 calls out, "Please help me. I think my arm is broken." The EMT then begins rendering aid. Another EMT approaches patient 2 and begins treatment. The patient, although competent and capable of objecting, expresses no objections to the EMT's ministrations. A third EMT immediately evaluates the condition of patient 3, who is unconscious, and begins treatment.

Exercise. Describe the form, or means, of consent given by each of these patients.

5.4 SCOPE OF CONSENT

If a competent patient has a right to consent to treatment, then it follows that the same patient also has a right to limit the scope of that consent or to withdraw consent once consent has been given. Patient limitations on the scope of EMS intervention arise regularly in two situations that are unique to prehospital care: (1) limitations on treatment and (2) limitations on transport.

Some patients seek to authorize, or consent to, transport only, without any active medical treatment. Without patient consent to treatment, an EMT cannot intercede medically. Thus, should the EMT accept this limited consent and transport the patient without treating? In such a complicated situation, the EMT should contact medical control immediately. Often, medical control can convince the patient to consent to treatment as well as to transport. If medical control intervention is unsuccessful, then the most prudent course of action for the EMT is to transport even if treatment is unauthorized. Once the patient is admitted to the hospital, then, generally, definitive care will be authorized and given because a formal medical environment often influences a patient. If the EMT treats the patient without consent, the patient may have a claim for medical assault and battery. However, an EMT may be better able to defend a claim for assault and battery than a claim resulting from serious injury or death.

Another problem EMTs encounter often is a patient who seeks to override local protocol by requesting transport to a different hospital. All legally capable patients have the right to decide where they wish to be transported. Whether local protocol or patient choice takes priority is determined by the circumstances of the particular case. For example, if a clearly competent patient elects to be transported to hospital B rather than hospital A, then that person's wishes must be observed. However, if the patient's decision involves transport to a distant hospital, that decision may deprive the local system of its only ambulance and the EMT may be reluctant to comply with the patient's decision. One solution to this problem is to transport to the local hospital and make immediate arrangements to transfer the patient to the selected hospital. This solution meets both EMS and patient needs. The patient may still have grounds to pursue a claim for the unauthorized transport, but the patient's damages will be minimized by the immediate transfer.

In situations involving patients who seek to limit the scope of consent, EMTs should minimize patient injury but respect the patient's right to refuse or limit treatment. In situations involving difficult patients, EMTs have a duty to educate the patient about the risks of limited consent or refusal so that the patient can make an informed decision and the EMT can protect against future lawsuits.

5.5 REFUSAL OF TREATMENT

Just as patients have the right to consent to treatment, they also have the right to refuse treatment. Many of the same rules that apply to consent also apply to refusal.

5.5.1 General Rules of Refusal

The general rules of refusal are similar to the general rules of consent. An EMT's course of action is dictated by the patient's competence and condition. If an EMT determines in his or her best medical judgment that the patient is incompetent—that is, incapable of assessing the nature and consequences of refusing treatment or transport—and a life- or health-threatening emergency exists, then the EMT may initiate treatment despite the patient's attempted refusal. In such a situation, the law implies consent because an emergency exists and authorizes the EMT to proceed. The patient is deemed incapable of refusing; thus, the attempted refusal is invalid. However, the EMT must show that an emergency actually existed at the time treatment was rendered. If an emergency does not exist, then the incompetent patient cannot be treated without the consent of someone authorized to consent on the patient's behalf.

A competent patient who refuses lifesaving or health-saving intervention presents a more difficult problem. An EMT has no right to intercede in such a situation. However, the EMT must determine if the patient is, in fact, competent. Serious illness or injury may have affected the patient's capacity to evaluate the circumstances of his or her condition. The patient whom the EMT determines to be competent has the absolute right to refuse treatment and transport.

Another problem sometimes encountered by EMTs is a patient who refuses treatment on religious grounds. Generally, the patient will refuse blood or blood products. The courts tend to respect the patient's right to refuse treatment on religious grounds unless overriding considerations weigh in favor of treatment. For example, if a patient is pregnant and a blood transfusion is necessary to save the mother and the baby, a court may allow this lifesaving treatment. Without these overriding considerations, however, intervention is unauthorized.

Some states specifically recognize a patient's right to refuse treatment on religious grounds. A Utah law provides that the state's Emergency Medical Services Act does not authorize "any medical treatment or transportation of a person who objects thereto on religious grounds."[4] The EMT who encounters a religious refusal should attempt to respect the patient's wishes. If the patient consents to limited treatment and transport but not to intravenous (IV) therapy, for example, the EMT should treat to the degree authorized but refrain from starting the IV. As always, the EMT should contact medical control for advice.

5.5.2 To Treat or Not to Treat: Weighing Liability Risks

When faced with the decision to initiate lifesaving treatment despite a competent patient's refusal, an EMT must weigh the risks. The EMT can either treat or not treat the refusing patient. To treat means to act in opposition to the patient's express wishes. The failure to treat may cause the patient to suffer serious injury or death. Because each situation is different and there are no clear-cut rules to follow, perhaps the best way to develop policies for dealing with patients who refuse treatment is to assess the types of lawsuits that may be brought under various circumstances.

An EMT who treats and transports a patient who has expressly refused such assistance may be named in a medical assault and battery or false imprisonment lawsuit. On the other hand, if the patient is abandoned as a result of the refusal and later dies or becomes seriously injured, the EMT may be named in a professional negligence lawsuit. If the EMT acted responsibly and reasonably under the circumstances, a jury is much less likely to find liability in the assault and battery or false imprisonment case than in the situation of professional negligence. This is particularly true if the patient would have died without emergency medical intervention.

Common sense dictates that an EMT should treat rather than abandon; however, there are, of course, no guarantees that the EMT will not be sued. The EMT who errs on the side of the patient is usually in a more defensible position. As with every call an EMT runs, the nature and circumstances of the patient's condition and the EMT's actions should be thoroughly documented.

5.5.3 Special Categories of Refusal: DNR Orders and Living Wills

Do Not Resuscitate Orders

Do not resuscitate (DNR) orders, also known as "no-code" orders, present a difficult problem for the prehospital care provider. Such orders may be written on nursing home or hospital charts or may be telephoned by a private physician to an EMT at the scene of a medical emergency. A DNR order has the same effect as a patient refusal—it instructs the EMT not to treat a particular patient under the particular circumstances. DNR orders usually arise in connection with terminally ill patients.

Policies for issuing DNR orders vary among health care systems. Assuming local policies exist regarding "no-code" orders, the policies must be followed in issuing a DNR order. DNR or no-code orders issued in violation of local policies or in the absence of such policies may be invalid. The EMT who fails to treat a patient in reliance on an invalid no-code order may be guilty of abandoning the patient and may be liable for the resulting damages.

Because of the difficulty in ascertaining the validity of DNR orders in particular circumstances, an EMT should take the conservative approach and err in favor of treating the patient. If a valid written order—as determined by local policies—or specific instructions from medical control are unavailable, an EMT should attempt to resuscitate the patient. After the patient arrives at the emergency room, the emergency physician then can decide whether to cease lifesaving efforts in accordance with the DNR order.

Living Wills

Another special category of refusal is the living will, or patient directive, which allows a competent patient to advise health care practitioners of the desire to avoid the imposition of so-called extraordinary lifesaving measures. Recognition of living wills is provided for by legislation in many states. Generally, living will statutes grant patients who face certain incurable injury, disease, or illness the right to provide in writing their wishes that lifesaving efforts not be undertaken and that life-sustaining procedures be withheld or withdrawn. State law establishes the validity of this patient refusal document.

Requirements for a valid living will are set out in state statutes. For a living will to be effective, each requirement of the particular state's law must be met. These laws also provide for a means to revoke the living will. EMTs should consult a local attorney to determine if their states have a living will law and the specific requirements of that law.

When patients properly execute a living will, it is presumed to be their instructions regarding medical intervention. The patient is deemed to understand the fact of refusal and to accept the consequences of that decision. An EMT who fails to comply with a valid living will may face liability consequences because treatment of a patient who has a valid living will constitutes treatment without consent. However, some living will statutes provide EMTs immunity from civil and criminal liability for failure to carry out the patient's instructions. State law must be consulted to determine the consequences, if any, for violating a patient's living will directions.

5.5.4 Release Forms

Many prehospital care providers carry release or patient refusal forms to be signed by the patient who refuses treatment. If the patient signs such a form, is the EMT then immune from liability? In most cases, release forms are not binding on a court. However, such a form, signed by the patient, presents good evidence that the patient understood the nature and consequences of the situation and made a conscious choice not to be treated and transported. To be valid, the release form must be signed by a competent patient. As part of the process of accepting the patient's refusal, the EMT must make diligent efforts to educate the patient on the risks of refusal and encourage the patient to seek and obtain further medical care.

The validity of a signed release form usually is tested in the abandonment or refusal situation. For example, an EMT arrives at the scene of an incident only to find a patient who refuses treatment or transportation. The patient agrees to sign the release form and the EMTs leave the scene. Later, the patient suffers further, more severe, injuries. In a subsequent action for abandonment, the circumstances surrounding the signing of the release will be examined carefully. The patient, or patient's family on behalf of the patient in a wrongful death claim, likely will claim that the patient was incompetent and, even if competent, did not understand the risks of refusing treatment. The EMT's best defense to such a claim is to carefully document the patient's physical and mental status on the patient care report form. The EMT also should document the efforts made to educate the patient about the risks of refusal and encouragement offered the patient to seek medical assistance.

5.5.5 The Concept of Informed Refusal

Perhaps the most important rule an EMT can learn in connection with patient refusal is the concept of informed refusal. In dealing with a patient who refuses treatment, an EMT should follow the "E²D" formula: educate, encourage, and document. That is, an EMT should

- educate the patient about the need for further medical treatment and the risks of refusal
- encourage the patient to seek further medical treatment
- document extensively the facts and circumstances surrounding the patient's refusal and the EMT's efforts to convince the patient of the need for follow-up care

An EMT who follows this formula is not guaranteed immunity from a lawsuit for abandonment. However, by using this approach, an EMT will have done everything possible to assist the patient in understanding the nature and circumstances of the illness or injury. The patient then is free to accept or reject treatment and transportation on an informed basis and the EMT has thoroughly documented the consent process.

NOTES

1. OR. REV. STAT. § 109.640 (1987).
2. Utah Emergency Medical Services Act, § 26-8-11(3) (1988).
3. OR. REV. STAT. § 109.650 (1987).
4. Utah Emergency Medical Services Act, § 26-8-8(2) (1988).

Chapter 6

Abandonment

6.1 ABANDONMENT: DEFINED

Abandonment of patients is one common form of emergency medical technician (EMT) misconduct. Abandonment is the unilateral severance of the EMT–patient relationship, without reasonable notice, when further medical treatment is required. Patients, however, usually do not suffer injury as a result of abandonment, although apparently many EMS providers commit abandonment frequently. In this section, the concept of abandonment and ways to avoid it will be examined. The nature of the EMT–patient relationship will be explored and the proper ways to terminate this relationship will be explained.

Abandonment occurs when the EMT–patient relationship, once having been created, is terminated intentionally and unjustifiably by the EMT. Abandonment is determined by the nature of the EMT–patient contact and the circumstances surrounding the severance of the contact. The key to understanding the concept of abandonment is understanding when the EMT–patient relationship is formed, and when and under what circumstances this relationship can be ended properly.

6.2 FORMATION OF THE EMT–PATIENT RELATIONSHIP

When the EMT–patient relationship is formed depends on the facts and circumstances of a particular case. Certainly, when an ambulance arrives at the scene of an emergency and the EMT begins treatment, the relationship is formed. In situations where an ambulance has been dispatched but has not yet arrived at the scene, whether an EMT–patient relationship has been created is less clear. Some laws suggest that once the ambulance begins rolling toward a call, the EMT–patient relationship is formed. Other laws suggest that the relationship is not formed until the ambulance arrives at the call and treatment begins. Each case must be evaluated individually to determine whether the relationship has been formed. Consideration should be given to the hypothetical examples later in this chapter.

6.3 TERMINATION OF THE EMT–PATIENT RELATIONSHIP

Once the EMT–patient relationship begins, there are only three ways in which it can be discontinued. Keep in mind, however, that there is liability for abandonment only if injury results to the patient because of the abandonment. The EMT–patient relationship cannot be severed unless

1. the patient does not require further medical care
2. the patient terminates the relationship
3. the patient is transferred to another qualified medical professional

6.3.1 Patient Does Not Require Further Medical Attention

One circumstance under which the EMT–patient relationship can be terminated properly is when the patient does not require further medical treatment. Many times, an EMT will respond to a call where no one is ill or injured. There is no legal requirement that every patient seen by an EMT be transported to the hospital. In determining whether further medical attention is necessary, the EMT must exercise great care. The EMT, as always, has a duty to act reasonably in making such a determination. In considering the following examples, note when the EMT–patient relationship was formed and determine whether the relationship was severed properly.

_____

Field Incident Example 6-1

Facts. An advanced life support (ALS) EMT responds to a call involving a 37-year-old male patient complaining of pain, which the patient describes as feeling like indigestion. After taking a brief medical history without taking vital signs or further assessing the patient, the EMT concludes that the patient is having an attack of indigestion. The EMT does not recommend transport to the hospital but advises the patient to contact the personal physician if the pain persists. The patient is ready and willing to be transported. Five minutes after the EMT leaves the scene, the patient suffers a cardiac arrest and dies.

Questions. Did the EMT properly terminate the EMT–patient relationship or did the EMT abandon the patient?

Analysis. Without question, the EMT abandoned the patient. The EMT–patient relationship was formed when the EMT arrived at the scene and began actual evaluation. The EMT then determined that the patient did not require further medical treatment. In some circumstances, this determination would constitute a proper severance of the EMT–patient relationship. However, in this situation, the EMT did not obtain enough information to make the determination.

Before an EMT can evaluate whether a patient needs further medical care, a duty exists to obtain all information necessary to make such a determination. In this example, the EMT needed to obtain a full personal and family history because the patient's family may have had a history of early onset cardiac problems. The EMT also should have conducted a thorough examination and evaluation of the patient including vital signs and an electrocardiogram using the ambulance's cardiac monitor. Such an evaluation could have led to the discovery of cardiac anomalies. With the information gleaned from a complete history and physical exam, the EMT likely would have concluded that the patient required further evaluation at the hospital. Transport of the patient to the hospital would have avoided the abandonment and perhaps saved the patient's life.

_____

It is important for an EMT to remember that if he or she determines that further medical care is not necessary, such a decision is made at the EMT's peril. If it turns out later that the patient suffered an injury because further medical treatment was necessary, the EMT may be liable for abandonment. The EMT has a duty to obtain all information required to responsibly assess the patient's medical needs.

_____

Field Incident Example 6-2

Facts. While responding to a motor vehicle accident call, an emergency medical services (EMS) unit is cancelled on-the-air by a police officer at the scene who states that there are no patients with injuries who require an ambulance. The EMS unit notifies dispatch of the cancellation and returns to the station. Two victims of the accident require medical attention and suffer injuries as a result of the delay in receiving proper care.

Question. Are the EMTs in the responding ambulance guilty of abandonment?

Analysis. The first problem presented by this example is to determine whether an EMT–patient relationship was formed. The relationship may have been formed at the time the call was dispatched. However others might argue that a relationship does not form until an ambulance arrives at the scene of an accident. If an EMT–patient relationship has not formed, then it cannot be terminated. If no such relationship existed in this example, then the EMTs may not be guilty of abandoning the victims of the accident. If, on the other hand, the EMT–patient relationship did form, abandonment occurred at the time the EMTs in the responding ambulance accepted the word of the police officer, terminated the response, and returned to the station. Liability would follow for the injuries suffered by the accident victims.

This example illustrates interesting issues regarding the duties of the respective parties involved in a call and when the EMT–patient relationship forms. The ambulance service or dispatch agency that handled this call clearly owed a duty to the occupants of the vehicles involved in the accident. As discussed in Chapter 3 on negligence, liability would follow if the EMS provider or dispatch agency breached its duty, which resulted in injury. It is fair to say that in this example, the ambulance service or dispatch agency was negligent because it did not require the ambulance to continue to the scene so that the EMTs could personally evaluate the patients.

The police officer in this example also could be held responsible for the accident victims' injuries because the officer negligently cancelled the ambulance. Although it is common for law enforcement personnel to cancel ambulances, such a policy can be dangerous. Law enforcement personnel who are not trained in prehospital care are ill-prepared to make medical decisions. The duty of the officer in this example was to allow the ambulance to respond so that the EMTs could evaluate the patients and make medical determinations regarding patient well-being. Law enforcement personnel are responsible for scene control while medical personnel are responsible for medical control. Cancellation of the ambulance constitutes negligence for which the police officer and law enforcement agency are responsible.

In this example, whether the EMTs in the responding ambulance are liable for abandonment depends on whether the courts of the EMTs' state determine that a medical provider–patient relationship was established. The more persuasive argument is that no relationship forms until the ambulance arrives at the scene of an accident. Only then can the EMTs determine whether the patients require further medical attention. However, if the courts of the EMTs' state determine that a sufficient bond was formed at the time of dispatch, the EMTs' return to the station without going to the scene and obtaining sufficient information to determine the medical needs of the patients may constitute abandonment.

The EMTs may be liable for negligence, as distinguished from abandonment, for failing to continue to the scene. Having been dispatched, the EMTs owed a duty to the injured accident victims to respond to the scene. If the EMTs decided, after direct consultation with the law enforcement officer at the scene, to cancel and return to quarters, liability may follow for negligently failing to respond. On the other hand, if the EMTs' dispatcher canceled the ambulance, then the responding EMTs may not be liable. EMT duty to accident victims terminates when the dispatcher cancels the call.

Field Incident Example 6-3

Facts. A private sector EMS unit arrives at the scene of a medical emergency. The patient is located in a house and fire personnel are already on the scene. As the EMTs walk up the driveway, they are met by fire fighter/EMTs leaving the home who advise them that the patient is fine and requires no further medical intervention. No additional information is provided. The private sector EMTs make no efforts to personally evaluate the patient; they leave the scene. The patient suffers a stroke as a result of a delay in obtaining medical treatment.

Question. Did the private sector EMTs abandon this patient?

Analysis. Again, the issue of whether an EMT–patient relationship was formed must be determined. Arguably, when the EMS unit arrived on the scene, the relationship was established. Thus, the EMTs could terminate their relationship with the patient if they determined that the patient did not need further medical treatment. To make this determination, they needed to obtain all information necessary to evaluate the patient's medical needs. However, by accepting the conclusions of the fire department personnel, the EMTs did not obtain any firsthand medical information about the patient. If a direct evaluation of the patient would have led the EMTs to determine that further medical intervention was necessary, then they are legally liable to pay damages for abandoning the patient.

Acceptance of secondhand and thirdhand information about a patient does not satisfy an EMT's duty to obtain all information necessary to determine a patient's medical needs. The determination that a patient does not need further medical intervention is made at the EMT's peril. If the EMT is wrong and the patient suffers injury as a result of a delay in treatment, liability may follow the EMT in the form of a lawsuit for abandonment.

_____

6.3.2 Patient Terminates the Relationship

The second way in which an EMT–patient relationship can be severed is when the patient terminates the relationship. A competent adult patient can properly terminate the EMT–patient relationship—this is commonly referred to as patient refusal.

A competent patient, as discussed in Chapter 5, is one who can understand the nature and consequences of accepting or refusing medical treatment and transport. Such a patient can refuse treatment and, thus, terminate the EMT–patient relationship. It always is assumed that a competent adult patient who severs the EMT–patient relationship requires further medical intervention. If no further intervention were necessary, there would be no need for the patient to refuse treatment. The EMT then would rely on the patient requires no further treatment method of termination.

Field Incident Example 6-4

Facts. An EMS unit responds to the scene of a bar assault. The injured patron suffers from multiple head lacerations and a possible fracture of the left hand. The patient elects not to be treated by the EMTs or transported to a local hospital. The EMTs leave the scene noting on their report, "Patient refused." The patient later is determined to have sustained a subdural hematoma, which would have been prevented by earlier intervention.

Question. Are the EMT s guilty of abandonment and liable for the patient's head injuries?

Analysis. Whether these EMTs are liable depends on a number of factors. Only a competent patient can terminate the EMT–patient relationship or refuse treatment. Thus, the first obligation of the EMTs was to determine whether the patient understood the nature and possible consequences of accepting or rejecting the EMT's help. Because the call was to a bar, the EMTs needed to establish whether the patient was under the influence of alcohol. It also was important that the EMTs determine whether the multiple head lacerations were symptomatic of a head injury. An intoxicated person or one suffering from a head injury may not be competent to terminate the medical relationship between himself or herself and an EMT. All objective findings relating to the patient's ability to understand the nature and consequences of accepting or rejecting treatment then should have been documented in the patient care report form. If this patient were determined to be competent, then the patient could properly terminate the relationship. However, if alcohol or injury made the patient incompetent, the patient needed to be transported for further evaluation. Terminating an EMT–patient relationship under these circumstances constitutes abandonment. Under circumstances where the incompetent patient continues to refuse, medical control or law enforcement should be called for advice and assistance.

A competent adult has the right to refuse treatment and transport and terminate the EMT–patient relationship. However, two additional duties are imposed on an EMT who encounters such a patient: (1) the EMT must educate the patient about the possible risks of not obtaining further treatment and (2) the EMT must encourage the patient to seek further medical attention. Only after educating and encouraging the refusing patient has the EMT fulfilled all requisite duties. The failure to educate and encourage the patient may constitute abandonment if the patient would have accepted treatment or transport if given proper education and encouragement.

6.3.3 Patient is Transferred to Another Qualified Medical Professional

The third way in which an EMT–patient relationship can be terminated properly is when an EMT transfers care of the patient to another qualified medical professional. Usually this transfer of care is to another EMT or to emergency department personnel. However, an EMT is under a legal duty to transfer care of the patient only to medical personnel whose qualifications are equal to or greater than the EMT's. Consider Field Incident Examples 6-5 and 6-6.

Field Incident Example 6-5

Facts. In a tiered-response EMS system, an ALS ambulance answers a call involving a patient complaining of chest pain. After a thorough evaluation of the patient, the paramedics determine that the patient's condition is not life-threatening. They then call a basic life support (BLS) ambulance staffed with basic EMTs to transport the patient. Neither of the paramedics accompanies the patient during transport.

Question. Does the transfer of the patient from the care of ALS paramedics to a BLS transport unit constitute abandonment?

Analysis. Yes. The responding paramedics are under a legal duty to transfer care of the patient to medical professionals of equal or greater qualifications. If the patient suffers a reversible cardiac arrest during transport by the BLS unit and dies thereafter, then the ALS crew is liable to pay damages for abandonment.

Although it is common in many EMS systems to transfer care of patients from ALS to BLS units for transport, such a practice constitutes abandonment. Most of the time, the patient will suffer no harm as a result of the transfer to lesser qualified prehospital care personnel. However, the law suggests that such practices leave the EMS system open to a lawsuit for abandonment. If the patient suffers an injury that could have been prevented by ALS personnel during transport, the transferring ALS crew and the crews' employer will be liable for abandonment. The same result would follow if the EMT transferred care of the patient to a hospital orderly rather than to a nurse or physician.

Field Incident Example 6-6

Facts. An EMS crew transports a medically ill patient to a local emergency department. On arrival at the hospital, the crew transfers the patient from the ambulance stretcher to a hospital gurney. They then leave a partially completed prehospital care report form on the gurney and leave without informing the emergency department staff of their arrival or of the delivery of a patient. The patient suffers injury as a result of being left unattended in the busy emergency department for several hours.

Question. Is the EMS crew guilty of abandoning the patient?

Analysis. Yes. The EMS crew is under a legal duty to remain with the patient until transfer occurs. The EMTs are under a further duty to convey all relevant patient information to the medical staff that is accepting responsibility for the patient's care and treatment. In this example, the EMTs did not ensure that emergency department staff took responsibility for the patient. Moreover, the prehospital care report form left with the patient was incomplete. Thus, the EMS crew abandoned the patient by failing to transfer care to another qualified medical professional, failing to remain with the patient until transfer occurred, and failing to convey all relevant patient information to those accepting responsibility for the patient.

The two additional duties imposed on the EMTs in Field Incident Example 6-6 apply in all situations involving the transfer of care to another qualified medical professional. Thus, within the context of this proper means of severing the EMT–patient relationship are three essential requirements:

1. Transfer must be to medical personnel whose qualifications are equal to or greater than the transferring EMT's qualifications.
2. The EMT must remain with the patient until transfer occurs.
3. The EMT must convey all relevant patient information to those accepting responsibility for the patient.

6.4 CONCLUSIONS

Understanding the nature of abandonment is an important first step in avoiding its consequences. Once formed, the EMT–patient relationship cannot be severed unless the patient does not require further medical care, the patient terminates the relationship, or the patient is transferred to another qualified medical professional. No other methods are available to terminate the EMT–patient relationship.

Chapter 7

Who is Liable?
The Concept of
Vicarious Liability

7.1 WHO IS LIABLE?

The question of who is liable for an emergency medical technician's (EMT's) negligence or other wrongful conduct often is asked in prehospital care circles. One might think that only the EMT faces the liability consequences of injuring another. However, others, such as the employer or physician director, also may be liable for the actions of an EMT.

The concept of indirect legal responsibility, or vicarious liability, will be discussed in this chapter along with the public policy reasons behind this rule of law.

7.2 CONCEPT OF VICARIOUS LIABILITY

The concept of vicarious liability is the indirect legal responsibility that is placed on one for the acts of another. Assume X is negligent and Y is not. Under some circumstances, the doctrine of vicarious liability imputes, or attributes, the negligence of X to Y. Thus, Y will be legally responsible to pay damages for the negligent actions of X even if Y did nothing wrong, did not encourage the negligence, and attempted to prevent it. Although at first glance this concept may seem unfair, it is founded on firm policy grounds.

7.2.1 Employer Liability

The EMT is liable for his or her own acts of negligence notwithstanding the doctrine of vicarious liability. Under the doctrine of vicarious liability, however, an employer also may be liable for the negligence or other wrongful conduct of an employee acting within the scope of employment. An employee acts within the *scope of employment* when he or she furthers his or her duties owed to the employer and when the employer is or could be exercising some direct or indirect control over the employee's activities.

Field Incident Example 7-1

Facts. An on-duty EMT negligently treats a diabetic patient. The patient is injured as a result of this negligence. The EMT has never acted negligently before and generally is known as an excellent practitioner. The EMT's employer carefully monitors the EMT's activities and conducts regular educational programs that the EMT always attends.

Question. Is the EMT's employer legally responsible to the patient for the EMT's negligently inflicted injuries?

Analysis. Under the doctrine of vicarious liability, the law places indirect legal responsibility on the employer for the negligent acts of its employee EMT. Liability is imposed on the employer because the on-duty EMT is fulfilling employment duties in a situation where the employer exercises control over the EMT. The EMT is considered to be acting within the scope of employment. Thus, this employer is legally responsible for paying damages to the injured patient.

The patient must still prove all four elements of negligence regardless of the doctrine of vicarious liability. If the EMT is found to be negligent, so, too, is the employer. The employer is only negligent vicariously if the EMT is found negligent.

Field Incident Example 7-2

Facts. An EMT delivers a patient to a hospital located a few blocks from the EMT's home. After leaving the hospital, the EMT decides to drop by his or her home to visit the family. The EMT does not clear the original call but remains available by radio. Dispatch believes the EMT is still at the hospital and the employer has a policy specifically prohibiting personal errands. While driving home, the EMT collides with an automobile, which results in injuries to several people.

Question. Is the EMT's employer legally responsible to the victims of the automobile/ambulance collision?

Analysis. The employer is only responsible for actions that occur within the scope of the EMT's employment. If the EMT is engaged in personal business not sanctioned by the employer, then the employer will not be held responsible. This is because the EMT's actions are deemed to be outside the scope of employment.

In this example, the EMT was engaged in personal business. In driving to his or her home, the EMT took himself or herself out of the scope of employment, leaving only the EMT responsible for any injuries resulting from the EMT's negligence. Thus, the EMT's employer will not be indirectly, or vicariously, responsible for the injuries to automobile accident victims. It is important for an EMT to remember that, outside the scope of employment, the EMT will be personally responsible for the payment of damages to anyone injured as a result of the EMT's negligence. Note, however, that if an employer allows personal errands or a home visit approved by dispatch, the EMT then is acting within the scope of employment, thus subjecting the employer to vicarious liability.

In addition to being indirectly, or vicariously, liable for an employee's negligence, under some circumstances an employer also may be liable for the *intentional* conduct of an EMT if the intentional conduct is reasonably connected to the EMT's employment.

Field Incident Example 7-3

Facts. An EMT responds to a 911 call involving a medically ill elderly patient. The patient's condition is not life-threatening. The closest hospital is located three miles from the patient's home, hospital X, but the patient requests transport to a hospital seven miles away, hospital Y, where the patient's doctor is located. The EMT transports the patient to the closest hospital despite repeated protests. The patient later sues the EMT for false imprisonment.

Question. Is the EMT's employer indirectly liable for damages awarded the patient in the false imprisonment lawsuit?

Analysis. In this example, the patient only consented to transport to hospital Y and not hospital X. The nonconsensual, intentional confinement of the patient within the ambulance for transport to a facility not of the patient's choosing could constitute false imprisonment. Whether the EMT's employer will be liable to pay damages for the EMT's conduct depends on whether the court finds the actions of the EMT to be reasonably connected with the EMT's employment. If the employer encourages transport to the local hospital to get ambulances back in service more quickly or if the employer is aware that such practices regularly occur, vicarious liability may follow. However, if the employer encourages transport in accordance with the patient's wishes, vicarious liability may be avoided.

In essence, if a patient seeks damages from an employer on the basis of vicarious liability resulting from the EMT's intentional, rather than negligent, conduct, the court will examine the nature of the employee's conduct to determine whether the employee EMT exceeded the scope of employment. Consider Case Summary 7-1.

Case Summary 7-1

Case Citation. Nazareth v. Herndon Ambulance Service, Inc., 467 So.2d 1076 (Fla. App. 5th Dist. 1985).

Facts. Plaintiff claimed an employee of the defendant ambulance service sexually assaulted her as she was being transported in the defendant's ambulance. Plaintiff sued the ambulance service, contending it was vicariously liable for the employee's conduct. The trial judge dismissed plaintiff's complaint. The plaintiff appealed the trial court's ruling.

Court Ruling. The Court of Appeals ruled that acts such as sexual assaults perpetrated by employees generally are not within the scope of employment. The court noted the general rule that employers are not liable for acts of employees that are outside the scope of employment. Therefore, without an exception to this general rule, the defendant employer in this case would not be liable for damages resulting from the sexual assault. Because the court determined that this case fell within an exception to the general rule, it held the ambulance service liable for the damages claimed in this case. The court classified the ambulance service as a common carrier—one that holds itself out to the public as being engaged in the business of transporting persons for compensation and that offers service to the general public. A common carrier has a duty to prevent injuries to passengers resulting from the carrier's employees. The court, in classifying the ambulance service as a common carrier, ruled that the defendant ambulance service was vicariously liable for the damages resulting from the employee's sexual assault.

Analysis. This case highlights the notion that an employer may be liable even for the intentional acts of its employees. Care must be taken to ensure that all employees are screened properly and trained to avoid incidents such as the one in this case.

The EMT whose intentional conduct is found to be outside the scope of employment may be personally and entirely liable for the consequences of his or her actions. Additionally, the EMT may be required to pay any judgment with his or her own funds because most insurance policies exclude intentional conduct from coverage.

The concepts of vicarious liability apply to public, private, and hospital providers. The principles of governmental immunity may apply as a defense to public providers. If an EMT receives the benefit of a governmental immunity law, the EMT's employer may receive the same benefit. For example, a California law that grants immunity to EMTs for all but grossly negligent conduct specifically says that a public agency that employs an EMT is only liable if the EMT is found liable.[1] In other words, if a jury found the EMT grossly negligent, the EMT's employer would be vicariously liable.

7.2.2 Physician Director Liability

Under some circumstances, a physician director also may be liable for the EMT's wrongful conduct. For example, a physician director who negligently supervises an EMT may be liable for the negligent supervision that results in injuries caused by the EMT. Whether a physician director might be vicariously, or indirectly, liable for EMT misconduct is unlikely and depends on a number of factors. No specific cases have been found that directly address this issue. Physician directors, however, must be careful to adequately train and oversee any EMTs under their control because cases seeking to impose vicarious liability on physician directors likely will arise in the future.

7.3 POLICY REASONS BEHIND THE CONCEPT OF VICARIOUS LIABILITY

Several reasons justify the concept of vicarious liability. These reasons are predictable employee negligence, allocation of risk, and employer hiring practices.

In the employer–employee context, the principle reason for the doctrine of vicarious liability revolves around society's expectation that employees will act negligently while working for their employers. An EMT whose negligence results in injury generally is not in a good financial position to compensate the victim. However, employers are in a better financial position to compensate the injured victims of employee negligence because employers have the ability to purchase insurance for such compensation. Thus, in a case involving a victim of employee negligence and the employer who hires and controls the negligent employee, the law allocates the risk of loss to the employer rather than the victim.

In the employer–employee context, the allocation of risk of loss to employers encourages them to hire competent employees and to supervise them properly to prevent acts of negligence or other wrongful conduct. Similar benefits are seen in the physician director context. The possible imposition of indirect legal responsibility on the physician encourages careful selection and training of EMTs. Thus, physician directors are encouraged to be more directly involved in the systems they oversee.

7.4 VICARIOUS LIABILITY: CONCLUSIONS

The doctrine of vicarious liability imposes indirect legal responsibility on one for the negligence or other wrongful conduct of another.

Generally, an employer will be held liable for the conduct of its employees who act within the scope of employment. Public, private, and hospital EMS employers all can be found to be vicariously liable. In some cases, physician directors also may be liable for the injurious conduct of EMTs under their license and control. The primary justification for the concept of vicarious liability is an allocation of the risk of loss from the innocent victim to the employer or physician.

NOTE

1. CAL. HEALTH & SAFETY CODE § 1799.106 (West 1988).

Chapter 8

Records and
Recordkeeping

8.1 INTRODUCTION

Recordkeeping in the medical profession involves a substantial amount of time. Different types of records are created in reference to patients. In addition, patient records serve many important functions. In this chapter, the medical record as it pertains to prehospital care patients is examined. The purposes of medical records and who has access to them are discussed. State laws that address medical record requirements in connection with prehospital care providers are summarized. Finally, medical record use in litigation is explored.

Emergency medical technicians (EMTs) typically complete two types of medical records on patients they treat: (1) prehospital care report (patient care report) forms (sometimes referred to as "trip sheets") and (2) billing information forms. Although both are important, this chapter will focus on the prehospital care report form because it relates to the legal aspects of prehospital care.

The content of patient care report forms varies from system to system. Some states set forth statutory requirements for the type of information that must be contained in the forms. These laws also compel EMTs to complete a patient care report form on each patient treated. Consider the following EMS laws.

Haw. Dep't of Health Admin. Rules, ch. 72, § 11-72-22 *Prehospital Standard Medical Recordkeeping*:

> (a) During or immediately after the time of patient care, an ambulance patient care report form shall be prepared for each patient . . . [and] shall include . . . the following information, on a department-approved standardized form:
>
> (1) Patient identification/name;
> (2) Residence;
> (3) Date of birth, and age;
> (4) Sex;
> (5) Date and time call was received;
> (6) Dispatch incident run number;
> (7) Ambulance unit identification;
> (8) Crew identification;
> (9) Time of emergency vehicle departure;
> (10) Location of incident;
> (11) Time of arrival at incident location;
> (12) Patient's condition observed by arriving crew;
> (13) Preliminary impression;
> (14) Anatomical sites of injury or illness;
> (15) Degree of urgency or severity of patient's condition;
> (16) Aid or treatment provided by crew;
> (17) Time of departure from incident location;
> (18) Outcome or destination of run; and
> (19) Time of arrival at destination.

Cal. Code and Regs., tit. 22, div. 9, ch. 4, § 100164 *Recordkeeping*:

> (e) The EMT-P patient care record referenced in subsection 100163(a)(6) [subsection 100163(a)(6) requires a patient care record to be initialed for every patient contact] shall contain, but not be limited to, the following information when such information is available to the EMT-P:

(1) The date and estimated time of incident.
(2) The time of receipt of the call.
(3) The time of arrival at the scene.
(4) The location of the incident.
(5) The patient's:
   (A) Name;
   (B) age;
   (C) gender;
   (D) weight;
   (E) address;
   (F) chief complaint; and
   (G) vital signs.
(6) Appropriate physical examination.
(7) The emergency care rendered and the patient's response to such treatment.
(8) Name of the base hospital physician and/or authorized registered nurse issuing orders.
(9) Patient disposition.
(10) The time of departure from scene.
(11) The time of arrival at receiving hospital (if transported).
(12) The name of receiving facility (if transported).
(13) The name(s) and certificate number(s) of the EMT-P(s).
(14) Signature(s) of the EMT-P(s).

These laws, and others like them, compel comprehensive recordkeeping in prehospital care. Many EMTs are overwhelmed by the amount of information they are required to obtain and document on prehospital care patients. The gathering and reporting of this information, however, serves a variety of purposes. For the benefit of the patient and the EMT, it is important that the EMT accurately complete a patient care report form for each patient contact in accordance with state statutory recordkeeping requirements.

8.2 PURPOSE OF MEDICAL RECORDS

The patient care report form serves a variety of purposes including as evidence at trial. Because the patient care report form is created at or near the time of the call, the information it contains generally is viewed as reliable. One important function of this document is to record patient symptoms and history as well as the EMT's examination, findings, and treatment. Completion of this form creates a permanent record of the events surrounding the patient's care and treatment. The record also documents unusual circumstances, such as a patient's refusal of care. Should a dispute occur later, a properly completed patient care report form serves to substantiate an EMT's position.

Perhaps the most important function the patient care report form serves in prehospital care is that of transmitting information among health care providers. In many emergency medical services (EMS) systems, patients are transferred at least once to another health care practitioner. The patient may be transferred from an advanced life support (ALS) first responder to a basic life support (BLS) ambulance (although in many systems, such practice may constitute abandonment) or from a BLS ambulance to an ALS ambulance. Regardless of the number of prehospital care transfers that occur, the patient eventually is transferred by the ambulance crew to the hospital staff. In each of these transfers, the patient care report form serves as a tool to transfer information about the patient. The receiving EMS crew or hospital facility relies on the information contained in the report form to plan and implement treatment strategies for the patient. Although it may be difficult to complete the form before patient transfer, every effort should be made to do so to ensure continuity in care throughout the patient's prehospital and hospital course.

Another important function of the patient care report form involves quality assurance. The patient care report form serves as an educational tool for the EMT, the emergency service, and the physician director. Past incidents can be examined, treatment protocols changed, or EMS systems redesigned in light of information in the patient care report forms. Some states require quality assurance review of patient care report forms as a licensing precedent. The Massachusetts Emergency Medical Service Regulations, for example, require a monthly review of trip records in all cases involving ALS services.[1] The failure to provide a mechanism for these quality assurance reviews can result in the denial of a license to an ALS service provider. Any realistic attempt to provide quality assurance in an EMS system must involve reliance on patient care report forms. Some states require quality assurance record reviews by law. Consider the following statute.

Alaska Health and Social Services Regs., art. 2, 7 A.A.C. § 26.245
Reporting Requirements:

(a) A certified emergency medical service providing either basic life-support or advanced life-support outside a hospital must complete an approved EMS report form for each patient treated. The report form must document vital signs and medical treatment given the patient.
(b) A copy of the completed EMS form must . . . be sent to the sponsoring physician.
(c) The sponsoring physician shall periodically review the EMS reports he or she receives to determine the appropriateness of treatment given.

Laws such as this one mandate both the completion and review of patient care report forms for quality assurance purposes. Such reviews help an EMS system avoid legal consequences by identifying and correcting system flaws before they result in injury to a patient. For example, a quality assurance review of patient care report forms might detect a problem with a certain treatment protocol, either in the form of use or misuse. The protocol then can be changed or further continuing education conducted to avoid future problems. Use of the patient care report form to improve the quality of an EMS system is important to systems desiring improvement.

Patient care report forms also provide information for researchers. Although not used extensively for this purpose outside the trauma arena, patient care report forms contain a wealth of data on the nature and function of EMS systems. For example, the Dade County, Florida, study discussed in Chapter 1 relied, in part, on such records. As research in the field of EMS increases, so, too, will the value of prehospital care report forms. If the type of information required by the California and Hawaii statutes discussed were evaluated comprehensively in every EMS system, one could learn much about the nature and value of prehospital care.

8.3 ACCESS TO MEDICAL RECORDS

As in all areas of health care, an important question facing prehospital care providers is when, under what circumstances, and to whom can patient information be released. Prehospital care providers often are asked to provide patient information. However, whether a request for patient records comes from the patient or a third party, the request must comply with state laws that outline the rules of disclosure. The general rules that apply to disclosure of patient information by an EMS provider are discussed in this section.

All states agree that medical records are the property of the medical provider and that prehospital care report forms are the property of the emergency service. Often, the patient or a third party will seek access to the patient care record or to information contained in the record. Many states grant patients access to their medical records. If statutes do not exist, court case law governs access to records.

Generally, laws allow patients unconditional access to their records. An EMS provider is required to provide a patient with copies of the patient's medical records on request. However, other states restrict a patient's right of medical record access. For example, one state allows only the patient's attorney access to the patient's medical records. Other states make it more difficult for a patient to obtain copies of medical records by requiring that the patient formally request the records under the state's Freedom of Information laws. Before releasing copies of a patient's prehospital care record, an emergency service must check applicable state law to determine the rights of requesting parties. For the protection of the EMS provider, no records should be released unless the request for records is in writing and is in accordance with state law.

Because of medical record confidentiality, third-party access to a patient's medical records is restricted. Under most state laws, the patient has an absolute right to keep information contained in medical records private and this right can be waived only by the patient. For example, when a patient signs a form authorizing release of information to a medical insurance company, he or she voluntarily grants the third-party insurance company access to the otherwise confidential records. This is known as a voluntary waiver of the medical record privilege.

In some states, a patient can involuntarily waive the privilege. For example, when a patient files a lawsuit against a medical provider who may be liable for the patient's injuries, the patient involuntarily waives the right of confidentiality of those records that relate to the injuries claimed. In such a case, the defendant medical provider may obtain copies of the medical records relating to the injuries claimed to have resulted from the medical provider's conduct. Without a voluntary or involuntary waiver of the medical record privilege, a pre-hospital care provider cannot release patient information to any third party.

As with many general rules, certain limited instances exist when patient records and information can be released to third parties. Because of the need for continuing medical treatment, EMTs are authorized to give a copy of the patient's prehospital care report form to those to whom care is transferred. For example, a copy of the form should be given to the transporting ambulance crew, which, in turn should pass the record on to the receiving hospital staff. This record then becomes part of the patient's hospital chart and will assist health care providers in planning treatment for the patient.

Patient records and information also can be released to third parties under court order. For example, if the EMS provider receives a subpoena for certain records, the records must be provided. Only in these limited circumstances can patient records be released to third parties without the specific consent of the patient.

Authorization to provide a copy of the patient's written record to the hospital does not authorize the EMT to broadcast confidential information about the patient over the radio to the hospital. Only information that is not confidential can be transmitted by radio. For example, the patient's medical condition can be discussed but not the patient's name or other identifying information. Thus, an EMT only may broadcast the patient's sex and age as well as the mechanism and specifics of injuries sustained in an accident.

Some states regulate record privacy in their EMS laws. Consider the following rules and regulations.

Haw. Dep't of Health Admin. Rules, ch. 72, § 11-72-22 *Prehospital Standard Medical Recordkeeping*:

> (c) . . . Any data recorded, collected, or evaluated for the pre-hospital emergency medical data system shall comply with applicable federal and state guidelines and statutes relating to the privacy of medical data and a patient's condition.

Wyoming Dep't of Health and Social Services, Div. of Health and Medical Services, ch. 4, § 7 *Patient Records*:

> No person shall release a patient trip record without the patient's consent, except to a health care facility, a lawful court order, or the Division.

These laws make it clear that EMS records are not to be released except in accordance with state law. Failure to comply with state EMS laws, including those dealing with patient records, could result in penalties imposed on the EMS service provider. For example, Rules and Regulations, Wyoming Emergency Medical Services, ch. 1, § 5, provides the following:

> Any person who violates these regulations . . . is guilty of a misdemeanor . . . and upon conviction shall be fined not more than four hundred dollars ($400.00) or imprisoned in the county jail no more than six (6) months, or both. . . .

Because of a patient's right to privacy, disclosure of confidential medical records may result in a lawsuit against the disclosing party. For instance, the EMS provider who discloses either in the form of written records or over the radio patient information without consent may be legally liable to pay damages. The EMS provider's best defense against such claims is only to release patient information in conformance with state law. Before releasing patient information, the EMS provider should obtain consent, receive a lawful court order, or obtain a written opinion from the provider's attorney authorizing disclosure.

8.4 RECORDS, RECORDKEEPING, AND LITIGATION

Medical records are used regularly in litigation because the prehospital care report form is a legal as well as a medical document. However, the fact that a patient care report form may at some point be used to evaluate and process a lawsuit should not detract from its primary functions. Only a small percentage of all prehospital care report forms completed by an EMT will ever be requested or reviewed by a lawyer. Thus, the forms should be completed with the patient's medical interests in mind, not the EMT's legal interests.

The prehospital care report form often is used by an injured person's attorney to screen a potential claim of medical negligence. In evaluating a suspicious incident, the patient's lawyer will first obtain a copy of the patient care report form. The record is scrutinized to determine whether it supports the patient's claim of EMT negligence. The report that properly documents high-quality medical care is the EMT's first line of defense against a negligence claim.

It is difficult for an attorney to proceed with a claim when the medical record created at or shortly after an incident documents treatment rendered in accordance with the standard of care, which is not negligent. Thus, the EMT's best defense to a negligence claim is to provide quality medical care in conformance with the standard of care and to accurately and completely document the care given. Such documentation will not guarantee that the EMT will never be sued. However, the likelihood of a successful lawsuit will be minimized.

If litigation does occur, the prehospital care report form serves important functions for the defendant EMT. Because a negligence lawsuit may not be filed with the court until many months or several years after an incident, the patient care report form can serve as a memory refresher for the EMT. A properly completed form will help an EMT recall specifics about the incident. The record also serves as documentation of the events leading to the lawsuit. Thus, if the patient claims abandonment, the record may show that the patient was competent and refused treatment after being encouraged to seek further medical attention and being educated on the risks of non-treatment. If the form presents a comprehensive picture of the events surrounding the incident, the burden in a lawsuit may shift to the plaintiff to show that the written record is incorrect in its assertion of competence or refusal. This is certainly preferable to an incomplete record for which the EMT will be required to prove the information that is not documented. There is a saying in the law regarding medical records: What is not recorded is presumed not to have been done. For example, if an EMT gives a patient oxygen but forgets to check the O_2 box on the patient's record, the law will presume that oxygen was not given. This places an almost insurmountable burden on the EMT to prove that oxygen was given in the face of the EMT's own report that indicates it was not.

Additionally, a poor record will subject the EMT to much embarrassment during a deposition or during trial when the plaintiff's lawyer stands up and argues to a jury that poor recordkeeping means poor patient care. Taking time to properly complete a patient care report form pays off in the event of litigation.

Once a record is completed, it must never be altered. Changing a medical record means suicide in litigation. The ethical implications are similarly traumatic. For example, in one case, a podiatrist was sued for negligence. The plaintiff's lawyer suspected that the podiatrist altered the patient's record after he was sued. After obtaining the original record, the lawyer sent it to an expert in document examination. The expert, using sophisticated techniques, determined that the ink used in the suspicious entry was not invented until some time after the date of the entry. Needless to say, the case settled shortly thereafter.

Maintaining thorough and accurate records of each prehospital care incident should be the goal of every EMS provider. EMTs should be required to complete a prehospital care report form for all patients. These records should be reviewed regularly for standard of care compliance and for completeness. Such a policy improves patient care and reduces the potential for litigation.

NOTE

1. Dep't of Pub. Health Regs., 105 C.M.R. § 170.986.

Chapter 9

Quality Assurance Programs
The Key to Litigation Prevention

9.1 QUALITY ASSURANCE PROGRAMS: A DESCRIPTION

Many times problems within a prehospital care system go unrecognized or uncorrected—improperly screened calls, basic life support (BLS) vehicles sent on advanced life support (ALS) calls, drivers speeding, treatment protocols ignored or followed inappropriately, and hospitals being bypassed improperly. If system defects result in injury to a patient because of negligence that is preventable but not prevented, litigation may follow. Quality assurance programs offer the best means for preventing litigation by identifying and correcting system flaws before they result in injury. Quality assurance has the specific and objective goal of positively affecting patient care. Quality assurance should reduce death and serious injury resulting from system defects.

Quality assurance programs have two components: (1) an identification element and (2) an active element. A quality assurance program first identifies problems within a prehospital care system and then actively seeks to correct those identifiable flaws. An effective quality assurance program should operate to screen a prehospital care system at many levels. Each and every component of an emergency medical services (EMS) system must be subjected to continuous and intense examination. Only in this way can system flaws be identified and corrected.

A quality assurance program should assure, at the very least, that prehospital care providers have written medical policies and procedures, on-line medical control, case evaluation and review mechanisms, continuing education programs, and data collection and evaluation mechanisms.

9.2 MEDICAL CONTROL

In prehospital care systems, especially those that offer ALS services, medical control is the foundation of a quality assurance program. EMS systems must be capable of providing on-line and off-line medical control. On-line medical control allows an emergency medical technician (EMT) in the field to obtain immediate medical advice either by radio or telephone while at the patient's side. The availability of on-line medical control may make the difference between quality and substandard care in a situation involving an EMT in a difficult patient care situation.

Off-line medical control involves general medical supervision of EMTs by a physician director who is experienced in prehospital care. BLS systems generally do not have physician directors. However, every state regulates ALS systems and requires physician direction. Consider the following statutes.

Joint Rules of the Iowa Dep't of Pub. Health and Board of Medical Examiners, § 470-132.9, Service Program—Medical Direction.

§ 132.9(1) The medical director shall be responsible for providing appropriate medical direction and overall supervision of the medical aspects of the service program. . . .

Illinois requires physician direction for each EMS system within the state. Consider the following detailed list of responsibilities placed on a medical director in an Illinois EMS system.

Ill. Admin. Code, tit. 77: Public Health, ch. 1: Dep't of Pub. Health, subchapter f: Emergency Services and Highway Safety:

§ 535.230 (b) The Project Medical Director will be responsible for:

1) Developing standard orders, (treatment protocols, Standard Operating Procedures), to be used in the EMS system.
2) Developing a list of drugs and equipment to be utilized by the EMS personnel in the field and to be carried on the EMS vehicles.
3) Obtaining and keeping current all necessary system approvals.
4) Coordinating the didactic and clinical experience of the EMS personnel in the system.
5) Keeping experience records on all EMS personnel and for collecting pertinent program data.
6) Be responsible for the supervision of all personnel involved in the EMS System Program.
7) Designating a physician to supervise the system in his/her absence.

In an EMS system that grants broad powers to a physician director, the director is responsible for all aspects of medical control and is required to ensure that the EMS system complies with the law. Punitive measures are available to directors to ensure compliance. Under Illinois law, the project medical director is specifically granted the authority to take drastic action in the event system participants fail to meet the required minimum standards. The following Illinois law sets forth the scope of the director's authority.

Ill. Admin. Code, tit. 77: Pub. Health, ch. 1: Dep't of Pub. Health, subchapter f: Emergency Services and Highway Safety:

§ 535.230 (c) THE PROJECT MEDICAL DIRECTOR MAY SUSPEND FROM PARTICIPATION WITHIN THE SYSTEM

ANY INDIVIDUAL OR INDIVIDUAL PROVIDER WITHIN THE
SYSTEM CONSIDERED NOT TO BE MEETING THE STAN-
DARDS OF THAT APPROVED SYSTEM. . . . Grounds for
suspension may include:

1) failure to meet the education and training requirements
prescribed by the Department in this Part or the Project
Medical Director; . . .

3) failure to maintain proficiency . . . in the provision of
basic, intermediate or advanced life support services; . . .

5) during the provision of emergency care, engaged in dis-
honorable, unethical, or unprofessional conduct of a char-
acter likely to deceive, fraud or harm the public or that
constitutes a criminal offense.

Many other states grant similar authority to physician directors.
No ALS system is permitted to operate without physician direction.
Although not currently required, all BLS systems also should have
some form of formal medical direction to ensure consistent high-
quality prehospital care.

To be successful, quality assurance programs must employ physician directors who are knowledgeable about prehospital care systems
and are committed to high-quality care. Such individuals must be immune to political pressure and must be able to impose sanctions if
necessary. Only in this way can an EMS system reduce the potential
for litigation as a result of negligently caused and preventable injuries.

9.3 OTHER COMPONENTS OF QUALITY ASSURANCE PROGRAMS

In addition to medical control, a quality assurance program should
provide for regular case and record review with direct input furnished
to the responsible EMT. Review of actual care and treatment situations with physician directors provides an EMT with feedback that he
or she can apply to future incidents. Questions about treatment
protocols can be answered and specific problems explored during
these review sessions. This retrospective examination of prehospital

care incidents is perhaps the most effective means of preventing future on-scene problems.

An effective quality assurance program also should provide frequent opportunities for continuing education and training. Continuing education will keep prehospital care personnel abreast of all relevant changes in medical standards of care and will ensure that skills are maintained at optimum levels. Almost every state law relating to advanced prehospital care providers requires continuing medical education. Failure to obtain sufficient continuing education credits may result in the loss of certification.

Development of written standards and protocols also should be a high priority of a quality assurance program. Standards and protocols provide the blueprints for patient care in an EMT's community. The more complete the blueprints, the less likely errors will occur. The written standards and protocols, however, must comply with acceptable standards of care. Effective quality assurance mechanisms will prepare an EMT for most incidents and will serve to prevent negligent acts that may result in litigation.

9.4 CALIFORNIA QUALITY ASSURANCE MODEL

Many states have laws that set forth quality assurance requirements for prehospital care systems. For example, California's law on medical control is comprehensive and divides the quality assurance function into three categories: (1) prospective, (2) immediate, and (3) retrospective. Within each of these categories are specific enumerated medical control requirements.

Cal. Health and Safety Code Admin. Rule, div. 9, ch. 4, § 100163 *Medical Control*:

A local EMS Agency with an advanced life support system shall, in conjunction with its medical director, establish and maintain medical control in the following manner.

(a) **Prospectively,** by assuring the development of written medical policies and procedures, to include at a minimum:

(1) Readily accessible treatment procedures which encompass the EMT-P [paramedic] scope of practice.

(2) Local medical control policies and procedures as they pertain to the EMT-P base hospitals, EMT-P service providers, EMT-P personnel, and the local EMS Agency.

(3) Criteria for initiating specified emergency treatments, for use in the event of communication failure. . . .

(4) Criteria for initiating specified emergency treatments, prior to voice contact. . . .

(5) Requirements to be followed when it is determined that the patient is not to be transported to the hospital by ambulance. Such requirements shall include but not be limited to:

(A) Specific medical conditions where radio contact is required.

(B) Written reports, if the patient is not transported, shall be reviewed on at least a monthly basis by the base hospital medical director.

(6) Requirements for the initiation, completion, review, and retention of a patient care record. . . . These requirements shall address but not be limited to:

(A) Initiation of a record for every patient contact.

(B) Responsibilities for record completion.

(C) Responsibilities for record review and evaluation.

(D) Responsibilities for record retention.

(b) **Immediately,** by providing for direct voice control by an EMT-P base hospital physician or an authorized registered nurse.

(c) **Retrospectively,** by providing for organized evaluation and continuing education for EMT-P personnel. This shall include, but not be limited to:

(1) Review by a base hospital physician or authorized registered nurse of the appropriateness and adequacy of advanced life support procedures initiated and decisions regarding transport.

(2) Maintenance of records of communications between the service provider(s) and the base hospital through tape recordings and through emergency department communication logs sufficient to allow for medical control and continuing education of the EMT-P.

(3) Organized field care audit(s).

(4) Organized opportunities for continuing education including maintenance and proficiency of skills. . . .

California's quality assurance/medical control law covers virtually every aspect of a complete quality assurance program. Written protocols, off-line and on-line medical control, record retention and review, and continuing education all receive attention under the statute. In California, every local EMS agency that administers an ALS program is required to implement medical control in every area outlined. This law can serve as a model for other states.

An EMS system that complies strictly with this law is much less likely to face the prospect of a lawsuit than one that does not. Field providers will be well educated, have adequate policies and procedures to follow, and have adequate on- and off-line medical control available when the need arises. Under these circumstances, field paramedics are much less likely to commit errors that result in injury.

9.5 DATA COLLECTION AND EVALUATION

One area of quality assurance programs that receives scant attention is that of data collection and evaluation. Few states have laws that deal with this area of quality assurance. Implemented properly, data collection and evaluation programs provide a means of assessing the impact, if any, of prehospital care systems on patient outcome. Data collected can assist EMS administrators in identifying areas of an EMS system that require change to improve overall patient outcome. An example of a prehospital care data collection and evaluation law follows.

Ill. Admin. Code, tit. 77: Pub. Health ch. 1: Dep't of Pub. Health, subchapter f: Emergency Services and Highway Safety § 535.700 *Data Collection and Evaluation*:

(a) All agencies providing pre-hospital care in the State of Illinois shall participate in an Emergency Medical Data Collection System. . . .

(f) The evaluation parameters of the Emergency Medical Data Collection System shall assess the systems' impact on death and disability. . . .

Illinois has made a conscious effort to determine the effectiveness of its EMS systems throughout the state. Armed with this information, EMS administrators can assess the impact of local EMS programs. Where problems are identified, changes can be made to avoid future problems or complications. Most importantly, where system flaws are identified, such flaws can be corrected before they result in injury. In this way, data collection and evaluation programs reduce the potential for litigation.

9.6 QUALITY ASSURANCE: CONCLUSIONS

Many EMS systems choose, for political reasons, to ignore system flaws and allow potentially dangerous conditions to remain. In some systems, treatment protocols remain outdated or nonexistent and untrained dispatchers continue to be responsible for screening and dispatching calls for emergency assistance. Additionally, hospitals incapable of handling certain critical patients receive such patients, multiple providers continue to battle over patients, medical control remains unavailable, and quality assurance efforts do not exist.

Negligent EMS systems will cause injury to innocent patients and will be sued. Such systems will discover that politics does not justify negligence. Negligence, however, does justify litigation. If EMS systems lack the political will to correct EMS system defects, the legal system will provide its own retrospective form of quality assurance.[1]

NOTE

1. R.A. Lazar, "The Legal System as a Form of Quality Assurance," *Journal of Emergency Medical Services* 11, no. 5 (May 1986): 6.

Chapter 10

Insurance

10.1 INSURANCE: AN ESSENTIAL ASSET

Insurance is an essential asset for any prehospital care provider and for those services that employ prehospital care providers. Although a comprehensive discussion of insurance and insurance contracts is beyond the scope of this book, certain critical elements of this topic will be examined because of its importance to prehospital care law. In the event of an incident that leads to a lawsuit because a patient or other person is injured by an emergency medical technician (EMT), insurance is often relied upon to defend the EMT and to pay any damages recovered by the injured person.

10.2 DEFINITIONS

Generally, an insurance arrangement arises when two parties enter into a contract in which one agrees to pay the other if a certain incident occurs. Sometimes it is difficult to determine if a particular incident is covered and how much coverage is available. The following definitions should help the emergency medical services (EMS) provider understand an insurance policy.

- An *insurance policy* is a contract under the terms of which the insurer agrees, upon payment of a specified premium, to compensate the insured upon the happening of certain agreed events or losses.
- The *insurer* usually is an insurance company and is the party that agrees to compensate the other upon the happening of certain agreed events or losses.
- The *insured* is the party or parties which, upon payment of a specified amount, expect to be compensated upon the happening of certain events or losses.
- The *insurance premium* is the amount the insured agrees to pay for an insurance policy.
- *Risks or perils* are the losses or events insured against.

An insured purchases an insurance policy from an insurer by paying an insurance premium. Under the terms of an insurance policy, the insurance company is liable to pay certain amounts upon the happening of any event insured against. For example, under the terms of an automobile insurance policy, the insurance company may be liable to pay damages resulting from injuries sustained in an automobile accident involving the insured's automobile.

10.3 INSURANCE POLICY PROVISIONS

Most prehospital care providers and some individual EMTs purchase insurance as protection against lawsuits. If there were no risk of an EMS provider or employee injuring another person or being sued, there would be no reason for insurance. Insurance allocates the risk of loss, at least to the degree insured against, from the provider or employee to the insurance company. In the event of a successful lawsuit, the insurance company pays the damages and costs of defense up to the limits of the insurance policy. The provider only is responsible for paying the premium and any deductible applicable to the given loss.

It is important that the EMS provider assess insurance needs on an ongoing basis. In assessing insurance needs, the EMS provider should be aware of the various components of a common prehospital care insurance policy. These include, but are certainly not limited to,

- the types of risks insured against
- the persons or entities covered by the terms of the insurance policy
- the limits of liability

10.3.1 Types of Risks Insured Against

Three types of insurance coverage are of importance to the pre-hospital care industry: (1) general liability, (2) business auto and (3) professional liability. General liability coverage obligates the insurer to pay sums for bodily injury and property damage resulting from an accident, which occurs as a result of the insured's business activities. For example, if a person (not an employee) falls and is injured during a visit to an ambulance station, general liability insurance would pay the person's medical expenses, wage loss, and other damages sustained as a result of the fall. General liability insurance does not cover claims that arise from automobile accidents or from injury resulting from the provision of professional health care services. In other words, general liability insurance does not cover claims of professional negligence.

Business auto coverage generally insures against damages that arise because of bodily injury or property damage resulting from an accident involving the insured's automobiles or ambulances. Thus, in the event of an ambulance collision, business auto insurance pays the medical and other expenses of those nonemployees injured in the accident as well as for property damage sustained by those non-employees. Business auto insurance also covers damage to the insured's automobiles or ambulances from collision, fire, explosion, theft, or vandalism. Business auto insurance does not cover claims covered by general liability policies or claims of professional negligence. Consider Case Summary 10-1, which illustrates the importance of having the right coverage for the right claims.

Case Summary 10-1

Case Citation. Newman v. St. Paul Fire and Marine Insurance Company, 456 So.2d 40 (Ala. 1984).

Facts. An ambulance operated by Jim's Ambulance Service accepted a call to transport a patient to a Mobile infirmary. During transport, the patient required oxygen, which initially was provided. However, the oxygen tank ran out before the ambulance reached the infirmary. Although another oxygen tank was available, the ambulance attendant did not begin using it. According to the ambulance attendant, approximately two minutes after the oxygen ran out, the patient stopped breathing. Despite cardiopulmonary resuscitation, the patient died. The patient's husband then sued the ambulance service, claiming the failure to provide oxygen resulted in the patient's death.

The ambulance company, which apparently did not have professional liability insurance, made a claim under its auto policy. The ambulance service's insurance company refused to accept responsibility to defend the subsequent negligence lawsuit or to pay any awarded damages, claiming that the patient's death did not result from an accident in which an automobile was used as required under the terms of the company's automobile liability policy.

Court Ruling. Interpreting the policy's language, the court concluded that the ambulance service's automobile liability did not cover acts of professional negligence, such as the failure to provide oxygen to a patient. The insurance company, therefore, was not required to accept monetary responsibility for the claim. The ambulance company would have to pay awarded damages.

Analysis. This case highlights the risk a provider takes in not carrying professional liability insurance coverage. Without the protection of insurance, Jim's Ambulance Service will be required to pay any judgment out of its own pocket.

It is important that EMS providers carry insurance to protect against all likely risks. A professional liability claim is likely for a BLS or ALS provider. A large judgment entered against an uninsured provider carries the risk of putting the provider out of business. The purchase of insurance should be viewed as a necessity not an option.

The most important insurance for the field EMT is professional liability coverage. Professional liability coverage generally insures against damages resulting from an error or omission committed by an insured EMT or paramedic during the provision of professional services. Acts of negligence generally are covered under professional liability policies. When an EMT is sued for failing to properly follow treatment protocols, professional liability insurance would pay any damages awarded and pay the costs of defending the EMT.

10.3.2 Persons or Entities Covered under the Insurance Policy

The second component of insurance coverage relates to those persons or entities who are covered by the terms of the insurance contract. Generally, the person who or entity that purchases the insurance is covered by its terms. Thus, if ABC Ambulance Service buys an insurance policy, ABC Ambulance Service will be protected by the policy's terms. If a paramedic purchases his or her own insurance policy, that paramedic will be covered by its terms.

More complicated is the situation in which an employee EMT of an insured ambulance service seeks the protection of the employer's insurance policy. Employees generally are covered under the terms of their employer's insurance policy as long as they act within the scope of employment (*see* 7.2.1). Under the terms of a business auto policy, for example, an EMT who negligently runs a red light in an ambulance and collides with another vehicle probably will be covered by the EMT's employer's insurance. However, an EMT who intentionally backs the ambulance into another vehicle undoubtedly will lose the protection of the employer's insurance policy.

10.3.3 Limits of Liability

Each insurance policy contains a limit of liability, or the maximum amount of money the insurer is obligated to pay for each event insured against. For example, if the liability limits of a professional liability policy are $100,000, the insurance company's liability is limited to that amount. Any judgment over and above that amount is the personal responsibility of the insured prehospital care provider or EMT.

10.3.4 Individual Insurance Coverage for EMTs

The insurance question most asked by practicing EMTs is: Do I obtain a personal professional liability policy or rely upon my employer's policy for professional liability coverage? To determine if personal insurance is necessary, the EMT must first answer the following questions:

- Does the employer have professional liability insurance?
- If the employer has professional liability insurance, is the EMT covered under the policy's terms?
- What are the policy limits of the employer's insurance?

If the employer does not have professional liability coverage or if the EMT is not covered under the terms of the employer's policy, the EMT should investigate purchasing his or her own insurance policy. If coverage exists and extends to the EMT, the amount of coverage should be evaluated. If the liability limits of the policy are low, the EMT may wish to obtain his or her own policy with higher coverage. If the liability limits are high, there generally is no need for additional personal professional liability protection.

To get answers to these questions, the EMT must expressly request a copy of the employer's insurance policy or policies. Given the potential personal monetary exposure of a noninsured or underinsured EMT in a serious negligence action, it is not unreasonable for the EMT to request and review the employer's insurance coverage. However, such a request may be opposed by the employer, although the employer, if it is looking out for the best interests of its employees, should share the contents of any insurance policies.

Whether a particular EMT should obtain a personal professional liability insurance policy must be determined on an individual basis. If the EMT is adequately protected under the terms of the employer's policy, no additional coverage may be required. On the other hand, if no coverage exists or protection is limited, the purchase of an individual professional liability policy constitutes a wise investment.

10.4 STATE STATUTES THAT REQUIRE PREHOSPITAL CARE PROVIDER INSURANCE

Some states require that prehospital care providers carry certain types of insurance to protect the innocent patient in the event injury occurs as the result of the fault of an EMS provider. Consider the following state laws.

Wyo. Rules on Emergency Medical Services, ch. 2, § 3, subsection (a):

Requires an applicant for an ambulance service license to provide:

(x) A copy of a certificate of insurance showing in force and in effect insurance coverage for each and every ambulance owned or operated, providing for payment of benefits and damages at least in the amounts as follows:

(A) Liability coverage in the amount of $100,000 for each individual claim and $300,000 for total claims for personal injury or death with respect to any accidental harm arising out of any motor vehicle accident. . . .

Mass. Reg. Code § 105 (1985), *§ 170.225 Insurance*:

(B) Each ambulance service shall carry the following insurance coverage for each of its ambulances:

(1) A minimum of one hundred [thousand] dollars ($100,000) on account of injury to or death of any one person;

(2) Subject to the limit as respects injury to or death of one (1) person, a minimum of five hundred [thousand] dollars ($500,000) on account of any one (1) accident resulting in injury to or death of more than one (1) person. . . .

Wyoming's law clearly limits the insurance requirements to injuries that result from automobile accidents. In other words, ambulance services in Wyoming are only required to carry automobile liability insurance, not general liability or professional liability coverage. Thus, a patient who is injured as a result of an ambulance crash negligently caused by an EMT is guaranteed at least some compensation; however, that same patient who is injured because an EMT fails to properly follow treatment protocols is not. Many states that require insurance coverage for ambulance services limit the insurance requirement to automobile liability coverage. As a practical matter, however, many ambulance services carry both general liability and professional liability coverage in addition to auto liability.

The Massachusetts insurance requirements are somewhat ambiguous in the sense that the law is unclear on the type of liability insurance coverage required to be carried by ambulance services. Because the law pertains to insurance of "ambulances" as opposed to "EMTs," it is possible that automobile liability coverage is what was contemplated by the Massachusetts legislature. However, an argument can be made that ambulance services in Massachusetts are required to carry insurance coverage to protect against any injury or death resulting from the ambulance service. If this argument is true, then an ambulance service in Massachusetts is required to carry all three types of insurance: (1) general liability, (2) automobile liability, and (3) professional liability.

EMTs should check state law in their states to determine applicable insurance requirements. If questions arise, EMTs should consult a local attorney.

Chapter *11*

Governmental Responsibility for Emergency Medical Services

11.1 INTRODUCTION

Emergency medical services throughout the United States are controlled and regulated by state and local government with varying degrees of success. The degree to which governmental entities involve themselves in prehospital care systems also varies. A government's level of involvement often depends on the existing legal framework. In this chapter, the duties and responsibilities of government in connection with the delivery of prehospital care and the consequences that arise from improper administration are analyzed.

It also is important to understand the component parts of any prehospital care system. Emergency medical services (EMS) system design often plays an important role in the quality and efficiency of care delivered. These system components and some of the factors that should be considered when either designing or altering an EMS system are examined. Political considerations also are discussed.

11.2 GENERAL CONCEPTS OF GOVERNMENTAL RESPONSIBILITY

Emergency medical care may be administered at the state and local level. In determining whether a state or local government may be liable for the failure to provide EMS or for permitting these services to be provided in a negligent manner, it must first be determined if a duty has been imposed or undertaken by the state or local government. Remember—without a duty, no liability will follow (*see* 3.2.1). Without a statute, ordinance, or other written law, there is no duty on the part of state or local governments to provide or regulate EMS. However, all states now possess EMS statutes and many municipalities have local EMS laws. Many of these laws impose a duty on state and local government to provide and regulate EMS. Some laws mandate local control of prehospital care, while others place responsibility for EMS in the hands of state officials.

Historically, states have had the power to regulate all matters involving the health, safety, and welfare of its citizens. Medical services fall within this permissible range of a state's regulatory power. While many state statutes purport to regulate statewide, many authorize, and sometimes mandate, regulation at the local level. State law may compel local governments to regulate emergency medical care. The extent of the power of local government to regulate EMS is determined by the type of local government. Some states delegate to a city, county, or special service district. Each of these local bodies has a different scope of power, depending on existing statutes.

Although all states now have EMS laws, these laws vary in their approach to EMS regulation. Alaska and Hawaii, for example, place responsibility for EMS administration at the state level. Alaska Stat. § 18.08.010 (1986) states:

Administration. The [Department of Health and Social Services] is responsible for the development, implementation and maintenance of a statewide comprehensive emergency medical services system and, accordingly, shall
(1) coordinate public and private agencies engaged in the planning and delivery of emergency medical services to plan an emergency medical services system. . . .

Thus, the authority and responsibility for developing and implementing Alaska's EMS system rests with the assigned state agency, in this case the Department of Health and Social Services.

Similarly, the State of Hawaii takes this "umbrella approach" to EMS administration. Haw. Rev. Stat. § 321-223 (1984) states:

State comprehensive emergency medical services system, establishment. The department of health shall establish, administer, and maintain the state comprehensive emergency medical services system to serve the emergency health needs of the people of the State. The department of health in the implementation of this part shall plan, coordinate and provide assistance to all entities and agencies, public and private, involved in the state system. All emergency medical services or ambulance services conducted by or under the authority of the department of health or any county shall be consistent with this part.

Hawaii, too, has made EMS a state function. The duty to direct emergency medical care rests with the Department of Health.

California takes a different approach. The state, through its EMS Authority, is responsible for the planning and implementation of guidelines for local EMS systems. The law also provides for optional local administration of these systems. Each local EMS agency created under California law is responsible for planning, implementing, and evaluating the local or regional EMS systems in accordance with the guidelines set forth by the state EMS authority.

Oregon takes an even different approach. State law sets minimum standards. However, each of Oregon's 36 counties is required to develop and implement a local ambulance service area plan that comports to at least the state's set standards. Of course, a county may set stricter standards than the state. Oregon's mandatory approach to EMS administration places a heavy burden on local government. For example, OR. REV. STAT. § 823.180 (1987) provides:

(1) Each county *shall* [emphasis added] develop a plan for the county or two or more contiguous counties may develop a plan relating to the need for and coordination of ambulance services and establish ambulance service areas consistent with the plan for the efficient and effective provision of ambulance services.

State and local officials responsible under state or local law for administering an EMS system must carefully scrutinize statutes, administrative rules, ordinances, and codes to determine their specific duties and responsibilities. Meticulous compliance with the requirements of the law will assure high-quality care and help state and local government avoid liability for negligent system design or implementation.

11.3 LEGAL CONSIDERATIONS IN EMS SYSTEM DESIGN

Many different types of prehospital care system designs are in operation throughout the United States. Every EMS system is made up of component parts. How these parts are combined to make the whole constitutes the system's design. The ingredients of many EMS system designs are set forth in state and local law. For example, CAL. HEALTH & SAFETY CODE § 1797.103 (West 1988) states:

> The [EMS Authority] shall develop planning and implementation guidelines for emergency medical services systems which address the following components:
>
> (a) Manpower and training.
> (b) Communications.
> (c) Transportation.
> (d) Assessment of hospitals and critical care centers.
> (e) System organization and management.
> (f) Data collection and evaluation.
> (g) Public information and education.
> (h) Disaster response.

For a number of reasons, many system designs possess flaws resulting in a higher likelihood of patient injury. One common reason is that officials who are responsible for system design or implementation do not plan and consider carefully each component as it relates to another. Depending on state and local law, a municipality that allows an improperly designed EMS system to operate may face a lawsuit. To understand the nature of a municipality's potential liability, it is first necessary to examine the component parts of an EMS system. Each element of an EMS system is dependent on other elements for support. In other words, EMS system elements act in a symbiotic relationship with each other. In selecting from among the options available, government officials must be cognizant of the legal ramifications that may flow from given choices. A discussion of these various elements of EMS system designs follows.

11.3.1 Prehospital Care Markets

Prehospital Care Markets include three choices:

1. emergency market
2. nonemergency market
3. assignment of exclusive service areas

The prehospital care arena can be divided into two subcategories of patient markets: (1) the emergency and (2) the nonemergency market. The emergency market is represented by all patients derived from calls for emergency assistance, regardless of whether these patients require advanced life support (ALS) or basic life support (BLS) care. These calls may be generated through a 911 central phone system, a seven-digit emergency number, or through a fire or law enforcement agency. The nonemergency market generally involves transfer and invalid coach services.

Governments have a choice of assigning exclusive service rights or allowing free competition among multiple providers. Assigning exclusive service rights limits the number of providers authorized to service the patient population in a certain defined geographic area. Governments can regulate the emergency market, nonemergency market, or both. In deciding whether to combine or keep separate the emergency and nonemergency markets for purposes of regulation, government representatives must keep in mind certain factors. Both markets comprise a finite number of transports. Expensive equipment and personnel are required to render services to the emergency market, while less expensive equipment and personnel are required to provide services to the nonemergency market. Generally, profits from servicing the nonemergency market are greater compared with profits from servicing the emergency market. Because of the nature of the patient population, standards are more strict in the emergency market.

Most state and local governments that regulate prehospital care services only regulate the emergency market and leave the nonemergency market open to retail competition. Few systems regulate the nonemergency market and even fewer combine and regulate both. Although the number of municipalities that limit EMS providers is increasing, most EMS systems today do not assign exclusive service areas for either the emergency or nonemergency markets.

Most state EMS statutes mandate the regulation of prehospital emergency services. Many local municipalities wrestle with the issue of whether to assign the emergency market exclusively to a single provider or to allow multiple providers to serve the community. Limiting the number of providers in a community generally is more economical because the costs of furnishing emergency services are decreased. Moreover, because only one provider may be involved, prehospital care is provided more efficiently. Several factors contribute to this increased efficiency, including a single administrative structure, a single physician director who controls quality assurance, and minimal politically induced "turf battles."

Formerly, government was forbidden from restricting the number of service providers in a given area. This concept is known as *antitrust* or the improper monopolization of a market. Currently, with proper statutory authority, government has the absolute power to assign exclusive service areas to prehospital care providers without fear of antitrust or other legal liability.

In considering Case Summaries 11-1 and 11-2, note that the law of antitrust may have changed. These cases are presented as examples of court decisions in a variety of jurisdictions.

Case Summary 11-1

Case Citation. Professional Ambulance Service, Inc. v. Blackstone, 35 Conn. Supp. 136, 400 A.2d 1031 (Conn. Super. Ct. 1978).

Facts. Professional Ambulance Service asked the court to order the mayor of the town of East Hartford, Connecticut, and the regional EMS council to stop assigning one company as sole provider of emergency ambulance service in East Hartford on the grounds, among others, that such action would violate antitrust laws.

Before the mayor's action, three ambulance companies provided emergency ambulance service to the town of East Hartford on a rotational basis. The actions of the public officials sought to designate a provider other than Professional Ambulance Service as the sole provider of ambulance service for the "primary service area." The actions of the EMS council and the mayor were based on state statutes and state health department regulations.

Court Ruling. The court ruled that state law provided an adequate basis "for the promulgation of regulations creating the primary service areas, assigning one responder to each such area and limiting or restricting the advertising of those who would provide emergency services or personnel." Thus, such actions did not constitute a violation of antitrust laws.

Case Summary 11-2

Case Citation. Mercy-Peninsula Ambulance, Inc. v. County of San Mateo, 791 F.2d 755 (Calif. 9th Cir. 1986).

Facts. Mercy-Peninsula Ambulance, Inc., a California paramedic ambulance service, brought an antitrust lawsuit against San Mateo County, California, and certain medical care providers, challenging the county's award of exclusive contracts to other providers of paramedic services within the county. The contracts entered into by the county were granted on the basis of competitive bidding. The county granted these contracts pursuant to the California Emergency Medical Services Systems Act and the Prehospital Emergency Medical Care Personnel Act.

Court Ruling. The court ruled that state law provided a sufficient basis for the county's actions. Therefore, no antitrust violation occurred.

Results similar to those discussed in Case Summaries 11-1 and 11-2 have been reached by other courts throughout the country. Public officials who are considering exclusively assigning service areas to prehospital care providers must examine carefully state and local laws to ensure that an adequate legal basis exists so that antitrust and other legal liability may be avoided. Although most state EMS statutes, regulations, and rules grant state and local officials the power to exclusively assign service areas, a local attorney should be consulted to verify such power.

An adequate legal basis also must exist before a municipality may exclude providers from the nonemergency market. Consider Case Summary 11-3.

Case Summary 11-3

Case Citation. Romeo v. Board of County Commissioners, 64 Ohio App.2d 269, 413 N.E.2d 1210 (Ohio Ct. App., 1978).

Facts. The plaintiffs—a funeral home and its ambulance service—asked the court to stop the county from using its EMS ambulances to deliver transfer and invalid coach services and to stop the expenditure of county funds for such purposes. The plaintiffs claimed that the provision of these ambulance services by the county interfered with their livelihood.

Court Ruling. The court ruled that the county did not have the legal power to provide nonemergency ambulance services. According to the court, Ohio state law only authorized the county to provide "ambulance or emergency medical services." Ohio law defined ambulance as:

> [A]ny motor vehicle that is used, or is intended to be used, for the purpose of responding to emergency, life-threatening situations, providing emergency medical service, the transportation of emergency patients and the administration of emergency care procedures to such patients. . . .

Based on Ohio law, as it existed at the time of this case, and on the definition of "ambulance," the court ruled that the county could not provide ambulance services for nonemergency patients. Current Ohio law may lead to a different result.

Before seeking to provide or to regulate the nonemergency market, government EMS officials should examine carefully state and local law. Only where state and local government have the legally granted power to be involved in this area of prehospital care can action be taken to limit or restrict providers in this market. From a public policy perspective, government officials should keep in mind that the provision of prehospital care services represents a privilege, not a right.

11.3.2 Level and Type of Service Available

The level and type of services available include four choices:

1. first response services
2. BLS services

3. ALS services
4. transport or nontransport

In the emergency market, government officials must determine the level and type of prehospital care resources to be made available within a community or region. Levels of service that may be provided include first responder, BLS, and ALS. Decisions also must be made about how these levels will work together and who will transport emergency and nonemergency patients.

First responders generally are volunteer fire or ambulance personnel whose job it is to stabilize the patient until a BLS or ALS rescue or ambulance arrives. First responders generally are trained in basic first aid. BLS services generally involve personnel trained to the EMT-basic level who provide noninvasive emergency patient care. Typical procedures performed by BLS personnel include bandaging, splinting, basic first aid, and cardiopulmonary resuscitation (CPR). ALS services involve personnel trained to the paramedic level who provide the widest range of prehospital care services. ALS personnel can provide cardiac monitoring and defibrillation, advanced airway management, intravenous therapy, and the administration of certain medications.

Once a system identifies the quantity and level of prehospital providers available, a determination must be made on how these providers respond to calls. A tiered response system is one that possesses multiple levels of providers. First responders and emergency medical technicians (EMTs) within each level possess increasingly sophisticated medical skills and equipment. In a tiered response system, a first responder may be dispatched to a call along with a BLS or an ALS ambulance or rescue. Alternatively, a BLS ambulance may respond with an ALS rescue. A rescue is similar to an ambulance but does not transport patients. Throughout the United States, there are a number of ways in which the tiered response system is set up. Many systems do not use a tiered response but merely send a volunteer or paid first responder ambulance, BLS ambulance, or ALS ambulance to treat the patient.

Regardless of who responds to calls for emergency assistance, a determination must be made regarding who will transport those patients who must go to the hospital. In tiered response systems, rescues may respond first, stabilizing the patient for transport in a separately responding ambulance. In nontiered response systems, an ambulance both responds to the call and transports the patient.

Almost all EMS statutes authorize state and local officials to determine the level and type of EMS providers for a community. In designing this component of a municipality's EMS system, care must be taken to avoid a system design that is inherently negligent. Consider Field Incident Example 11-1.

_____

Field Incident Example 11-1

Facts. Local EMS officials design, or allow to remain in place, a tiered response system that authorizes ALS ambulances, staffed with paramedics, to respond to calls. If the patient requires ALS care, then the ALS ambulance transports the patient to the hospital. If, however, the ALS crew determines that the patient needs only BLS care, then a BLS ambulance is called for transport. The paramedics do not accompany BLS patients to the hospital.

Questions. Is this component of this community's EMS system properly designed? If not, could the local government be sued on the grounds that the system design is inappropriate?

Analysis. The described system design is inherently negligent. Once the ALS crew forms an EMT–patient relationship with a patient, the relationship can be terminated only in one way—by transferring care to a qualified medical professional who has equal or greater qualifications. The transfer of care from ALS personnel to BLS personnel, who are by definition less qualified, technically constitutes abandonment (*see* Chapter 6 for a complete discussion of abandonment). A system that uses this design is seeking to legally authorize patient abandonment. In a state that allows a municipalilty to be sued for EMS-related decisions, a municipality may be liable for implementing or allowing to remain in operation a system that sanctions patient abandonment where abandonment results in injury to the patient.

_____

In designing a tiered response system, state and local officials should evaluate carefully the effect of alternative levels of service and alternative mechanisms of response on patients. Before implementation occurs, local counsel should be consulted.

11.3.3 Dispatch and Communications

Dispatch and communications offers several choices:

- central dispatch center
- multiple dispatch centers
- 911 or seven-digit phone answering point
- call routing
  1. retail competition
  2. dispatch center distribution
     (a) call rotation
     (b) exclusive area assignment
     (c) closest ambulance
- call screening: yes or no
- on-line EMT/physician communications
- EMT/hospital communications

Another component of a community's EMS system that EMS officials must consider is dispatch and communications. The choices listed above must be examined in designing or changing this integral part of the EMS response system. First, EMS officials must determine whether the dispatch and communications center is to be centralized or decentralized. In some systems, each EMS provider has its own dispatch center. In others, the dispatch function is consolidated in one location. Factors such as cost and efficiency should be considered in decision making. Generally, the governmental decision to centralize or decentralize the dispatch function will not lead to legal liability as long as the decision is made reasonably.

Regionally, another factor to consider is the means by which calls for emergency assistance will be made by those people who require assistance. A growing number of systems use a 911 phone answering point; others use a seven-digit number. In many EMS systems, a calling party must choose among a number of providers, locate the provider's seven-digit number, and call. There are obvious disadvantages to this type of calling mechanism and obvious advantages to using a 911 phone answering point. Arguably, where 911 technology is available but not implemented, legal liability may result, if, for example, a delay in obtaining emergency assistance results in injury to a patient and the delay can be causally traced to the municipality's phone answering mechanism. Although this scenario is unlikely, such factors should be considered by EMS officials who are responsible for a community's dispatch policy.

Another important component of dispatch is call routing. This is the mechanism by which calls are allocated or distributed once they are received from a calling party. Throughout the United States, various forms of call distribution are used. The old-fashioned means of allocating calls is by way of retail competition. In systems using this form of allocation, the call is broadcast over the radio generally but not to any one EMS provider. All providers in the system then have an opportunity to respond, oftentimes racing each other to the scene. The patient then is handled by either the first ambulance on-scene or by the crew that wins the competition some other way. A municipality's potential legal liability is greatest in the old-fashioned system. A local government that knowingly allows this form of competition to occur may well be liable for the consequences of an ambulance crash or from injuries suffered as a result of this negligent form of system design.

Most commonly, calls are distributed or allocated at the dispatch center. In a system with multiple providers, each of which has its own seven-digit number, calls may be allocated simply on the basis of which provider is called. In a system with a centralized dispatch function, call distribution mechanisms vary. Calls may be allocated on a rotational basis, on the basis of exclusive service areas, on the basis of closest ambulance, or by some other criteria developed by the dispatch policymakers. Municipal liability may follow the negligent design of the dispatch allocation function. Consider Field Incident Example 11-2.

Field Incident Example 11-2

Facts. A community has two EMS providers: (1) one ALS and (2) one BLS. For political reasons, the administrator of the county dispatch center allocates all EMS calls on a purely rotational basis regardless of the nature of the call. No attempt is made at the dispatch center to categorize EMS calls as life-threatening or non-life-threatening. A cardiac arrest call is received. Both providers located an equal distance from the call location have ambulances available. Because the BLS provider is "up" in rotation, it is dispatched to the scene. Proper ALS care would save the patient's life. However, because the BLS ambulance is dispatched to the scene, the patient dies.

Question. Is the county legally liable for this patient's death?

Analysis. Depending on state law on the subject of municipal liability, the county may be liable to pay damages in this situation. The call allocation component of this EMS system is inherently negligent. The failure to send the ALS ambulance given the clearly life-threatening nature of the call constitutes negligence. If resources are available but a municipality fails to dispatch the provider most qualified to handle a given call, then that municipality may face civil liability consequences. To avoid liability, call allocation must be based on patient need—not on political concerns.

Systems that use the closest ambulance means of call allocation also must be alert because often a "favorite" provider may be given calls even though that provider is farther away. Such practices may result in liability if the time delay results in injury to a patient.

Overall, care must be exercised by officials who are responsible for the dispatch function to assure that calls are allocated based on objective criteria. Permitting an inherently negligent call allocation mechanism to remain operational may lead the municipality into the courtroom.

EMS officials who are responsible for dispatch also must decide whether to use some form of call screening. Call screening involves a mechanism for classifying calls on the basis of seriousness and then dispatching resources best able to deal with the particular call. A system also must elect whether to give pre-arrival instructions to the calling party. A system using pre-arrival instructions advises the calling party on treatment until the EMS crew arrives. For example, in a cardiac arrest situation, the dispatcher may advise the caller to perform CPR and explain how to do it.

Call screening and pre-arrival instructions, if used properly, will benefit the patient. Such practices ensure that proper resources will be dispatched to the patient and that some care will be instituted even before the EMS unit arrives. Because liability may follow if these methods are used improperly, EMS officials must adequately train and supervise dispatchers who use call screening and pre-arrival instructions. Moreover, care must be taken to assure that dispatchers have adequate policies and procedures to follow.

11.3.4 Types of Prehospital Care Providers

Communities may select from several alternatives in deciding the makeup of an EMS provider. These choices include the following:

- public provider(s)
- private provider(s)
- a combination of public and private providers
- quasi-public or third-service provider(s)
- paid or volunteer crews
- user funded, tax funded, or combination (public subsidy)

Public providers generally are publicly funded fire departments or public safety agencies. Private ambulance companies are another common EMS provider. Another less common entity is the quasi-public or third-service provider. The system design that uses the third service is sometimes referred to as the "Public Utility Model."[1] This model incorporates a competitively selected operations contractor and an overseeing governmental authority. Another important consideration for EMS administrators in designing a system relates to whether EMS crews are paid or volunteer and how the system will be funded.

Choices about who will provide EMS services in a community, whether the EMTs will be paid, and how the system will be funded constitute inherently political decisions. However, negligence liability may follow, for example, if EMS officials allow a knowingly unqualified provider to continue to operate in the community. As noted in 11.3.1, EMS officials also may be sued by a provider that is excluded from a particular market.

11.3.5 Transport Destination Decisions

The transport destination choices include

- closest hospital with emergency department
- trauma hospital
- contract hospital
- hospital that owns or operates the ambulance service

Transport destination policies are, from the patient's perspective, an important component of the community's EMS system. EMS administrators can develop procedures that dictate whether patients will be taken to, among other destinations, the closest appropriate hospital, to a trauma hospital, to a contract hospital, or to a hospital that owns or operates the ambulance service. Whether liability may follow from these policies often depends on whether the policies were developed with the patient's best interests in mind or were based on politics or economics.

In a community where all hospital emergency departments are equal, a policy that provides for the delivery of a patient to the closest hospital is reasonable. However, if certain hospitals are more qualified to handle certain classes of patients, policies should mandate that patients who meet requisite criteria should be delivered to the most qualified hospital. For example, political considerations aside, hospitals that are objectively capable of handling trauma patients should receive a community's trauma patient population.

Transport destination policies should never be based solely on economic considerations. Simply because a hospital operates an ambulance service does not mean that every patient transported by that service should go to the owner hospital. A municipality that allows such practices to exist may face liability consequences if, for example, a patient is injured as a result of a delay in reaching definitive medical care because an ambulance bypassed qualified hospitals to reach the owner hospital. As with every component of a community's EMS system, policies relating to transport decisions should be developed and implemented carefully.

Case Summary 11-4

Case Citation. Wideman v. Shallowford Community Hospital, Inc., 826 F.2d 1030 (Georgia 11th Cir. 1987).

Facts. The plaintiff, four months pregnant, began experiencing abdominal pain and called her obstetrician. The doctor instructed the plaintiff to come immediately to Piedmont Hospital where he was on staff. The plaintiff called 911 and requested that an ambulance take her to Piedmont. According to the plaintiff, employees of the county ambulance service refused to take her to Piedmont and instead took her against her express wishes to Shallowford Community Hospital, a hospital with whom the county ambulance service had a contract for payment.

Although she was later transferred to Piedmont, the plaintiff went into premature labor as a result of the substantial delay at Shallowford. After arrival at Piedmont, plaintiff's physician was unable to stop labor and the baby, born premature, died.

The plaintiff brought a lawsuit against the county ambulance service, claiming a denial of a contended constitutional right to essential medical care and treatment. She claimed that the county had a policy and practice of transporting patients only to hospitals such as Shallowford, which guaranteed payment of the county's EMS bills. She also brought nonconstitutionally based claims of false imprisonment, negligence, and intentional infliction of emotional distress.

Court Ruling. The Eleventh Circuit of the United States Court of Appeals let stand the trial court's decision to dismiss the plaintiff's constitutional claim. The court ruled that no general constitutional right exists that guarantees the provision of medical treatment and services by a state or municipality except under special circumstances. Because no special circumstances existed in this case, the plaintiff possessed no constitutional claim. In other words, the court concluded that a state or municipality has no constitutionally imposed duty to provide emergency medical care.

The court expressly left open the possibility that the plaintiff could recover from the county on her other claims. If the facts are as stated, the county may be legally liable to pay money damages for false imprisonment, negligence, and intentional infliction of emotional distress.

Analysis. This case highlights some of the legal pitfalls potentially facing a municipality that provides ambulance service. Transport decisions made by a county ambulance service's EMTs must be based on patient need. Transport decisions based solely on economics likely will lead to litigation and liability when injury occurs.

11.3.6 Miscellaneous Considerations

Other components EMS officials must consider in designing or redesigning an EMS system include

- protocols and standards
- quality assurance
- medical control

Taken together, these elements of the EMS system often represent the difference between quality patient care and substandard patient care. All of these factors are discussed elsewhere in this book but, suffice it to say, policymakers must assure that quality control mechanisms exist and are used. It is conceivable that a government may be liable for the failure to provide quality assurance checks and balances that are designed to avoid patient injury.

11.4 SOME THOUGHTS ON EMS SYSTEM DESIGN AND GOVERNMENTAL RESPONSIBILITY

Generally, a government is responsible for the health, safety, and welfare of its citizens. Certainly, EMS falls within the category of public safety. A government's involvement in EMS may be active or passive—that is, a government may actively regulate and participate in the delivery of prehospital care services, it may passively allow such services to be delivered unregulated, or it may passively permit the unavailability of emergency medical care.

A government's legally imposed duty to regulate EMS, if present, derives from a number of factors, most important, the state's EMS laws. These laws may place responsibilities on state or local governments to ensure the delivery of quality EMS. If a state or local law imposes an express duty on government to provide a certain level of emergency medical care, the failure to provide such care may result in a negligence lawsuit. For example, if state law mandates that each county in some manner provide ALS prehospital care to all areas of the county, failure to provide these services, which results in patient injury, is negligence. Thus, an express duty is imposed on the government to design a system that meets the requirements of state and local law.

If a government actively regulates or provides EMS, then it must do so non-negligently. For example, governmentally written and adopted treatment protocols must conform to medically acceptable standards of care. County owned and operated ambulances that are staffed by county employees must provide emergency medical care in a non-negligent fashion. A government has a duty to control the quality of each system component to ensure non-negligent operation.

If a government passively allows a negligently operated or designed system to provide prehospital care, liability may follow. Arguably, a local government that passively allows competition at the street level is negligent, because the potential for grave injury in such a system is great. For example, when the Company A ambulance races the Company B ambulance to the scene of an automobile accident, one of the ambulances is likely to cause or be involved in a collision that results in serious injury. The local government that allows such a system design to operate certainly has breached its duty toward its citizens.

In designing or operating a prehospital care system, each component must be examined carefully. Policies relating to call screening, dispatch, call rotation, unit availability, transport, medical control, treatment protocols, hospital bypass, and other components must be critically considered. A government that carefully designs its EMS system based on objectively identified needs and resources will decrease the likelihood of patient injury resulting from system design flaws and, in turn, reduce the potential for litigation. Although politics and political considerations play a pervasive, but often destructive role in EMS system design, public officials must always remember: Political compromise does not justify negligent system design, but negligent system design does justify a lawsuit.

NOTE

1. J. Stout, "Public Utility Model Revisited," *Journal of Emergency Medical Services*, Volume 10, no. 3 (1985): 71.

Glossary

ABANDONMENT. The improper termination of an EMT–patient relationship.

ADVANCED LIFE SUPPORT. Treatment rendered by highly skilled personnel, including procedures such as cardiac monitoring and defibrillation, advanced airway management, intravenous therapy, and the administration of certain medications.

ALS. *See* ADVANCED LIFE SUPPORT.

ANSWER TO COMPLAINT. A legal document filed on behalf of the defendant in response to the plaintiff's complaint.

APPEAL. A request to an appellate court that the decision of a trial court be reviewed and changed.

BASIC LIFE SUPPORT. Treatment rendered by personnel generally trained to the EMT-basic level, including procedures such as bandaging, splinting, providing basic first aid, and performing CPR.

BEYOND A REASONABLE DOUBT. Standard of proof in a criminal case requiring the prosecutor to prove guilt to a moral certainty.

BLS. *See* BASIC LIFE SUPPORT.

BREACH OF DUTY. In negligence law, the failure to conform with the minimum standard of conduct required under the circumstances.

149

CAUSATION OF INJURY. In negligence law, a reasonably close causal connection between the EMT's conduct and the patient's resulting injury.

CIVIL LAW. Laws designed to enforce, redress, and protect private rights. In essence, all law not criminal in nature.

COMMON LAW. The body of principles relating to government and society which derive their authority from society's past customs and practices. Courts rely on historical customs and practices to create legal common law principles.

COMPARATIVE/CONTRIBUTORY NEGLIGENCE. Negligence on the part of the plaintiff which may act to proportionally reduce or eliminate the plaintiff's damages recovery.

COMPENSATION. The payment of damages for injuries directly resulting from a breach of duty.

COMPENSATORY DAMAGES. In negligence law, damages intended to compensate an injured party for the injury sustained as a result of an EMT's breach of duty.

COMPETENCE. *See* MENTAL CAPACITY.

COMPLAINT. A legal document filed on behalf of the plaintiff that contains allegations against the defendant in a civil lawsuit.

CONSENT TO TREATMENT. The agreement of the patient to treatment or transport.

CPR. Cardiopulmonary resuscitation.

CRIMINAL LAW. Laws designed to prevent harm to society. These laws declare what conduct is criminal and prescribe the punishment to be imposed for such conduct.

DAMAGES. The loss or damage for which the law allows recovery.

DEFENDANT. In a civil lawsuit, the person or entity being sued.

DEPOSITIONS. The process of taking testimony under oath outside of a courtroom.

DISCOVERY. The process, during the pendency of a civil lawsuit, whereby the parties exchange information. Discovery generally involves the exchange of documents and the taking of depositions.

DNR ORDERS. *See* DO NOT RESUSCITATE ORDERS.

DO NOT RESUSCITATE ORDERS. An instruction directing the EMT not to treat a particular patient.

DUTY. The legal obligation placed on an EMT to conform to a minimum required standard of conduct.

DUTY TO RESCUE LAWS. Laws imposing a legal duty on the general public to aid persons in distress. Without such laws, no legal duty requiring anyone to voluntarily assist persons in need exists.

EMS. Emergency medical services.

EMT. Emergency medical technician.

EXCLUSIVE SERVICE AREA. A geographic area assigned to one pre-hospital care provider. Other providers are excluded from operating in an assigned exclusive service area.

FALSE IMPRISONMENT. The nonconsensual, intentional confinement of a person without some lawful reason for the confinement.

FIRST RESPONDER. Generally, volunteer fire or ambulance personnel whose job is to stabilize a patient until a BLS or ALS rescue or ambulance arrives.

GENERAL DAMAGES. A form of damages in negligence law. These damages generally include pain and suffering, emotional distress, and the loss of society and companionship.

GOOD SAMARITAN LAWS. State statutory laws protecting individuals who aid persons in imminent and serious peril from civil liability for injuries suffered by the victim as a result of the rescuer's conduct.

GOVERNMENTAL IMMUNITY. Historically, a rule of law prohibiting lawsuits against governmental bodies. These types of laws gradually are being modified or eliminated to allow such lawsuits.

GOVERNMENTAL IMMUNITY LAWS. Statutes setting forth the conditions and restrictions applicable to a governmental entity or employee sued for acts of negligence as well as other claims. These laws are referred to as Tort Claims Acts.

GROSS NEGLIGENCE. Ordinary negligence and gross negligence differ in the degree of inattention to a legal duty. Gross negligence constitutes the failure to perform a duty in reckless disregard of the consequences to another; the want of even slight care. It is conduct considered less than willful or intentional.

GUARDIAN. A person who is lawfully invested with the power of managing another person's affairs.

IMMUNITY STATUTES. Similar to Good Samaritan laws, prehospital care immunity statutes provide civil liability protection to emergency medical personnel for acts performed on-the-job.

INTERROGATORIES. A discovery device consisting of a series of written questions about a pending case prepared by one party and submitted to another party or a witness. The answers to the interrogatory questions are generally made under oath in the form of a signed sworn statement.

JUDICIAL PRECEDENT. Prior legal cases which are factually identical or similar to a case pending before a court. Courts attempt to decide pending cases on the basis of principles established in prior cases.

JURY INSTRUCTIONS. An explanation given by the judge to the jury of the rules and principles of law applicable to the case.

LEGAL CAPACITY. In consent law, a person who is legally qualified to give consent.

LEGAL CITATION. A means of identifying and locating a court's written opinion.

LITIGATION. All proceedings in connection with a legal action in which a person seeks to enforce a right or seeks a remedy.

LIVING WILL. A directive, prepared by a competent patient, that instructs health care providers not to perform extraordinary lifesaving measures.

MEDICAL ASSAULT AND BATTERY. The act of placing a patient in fear of being touched without consent coupled with the actual touching without consent.

MENTAL CAPACITY. In consent law, the ability of a person to understand the nature and consequences of authorizing treatment or transport. Also known as competence.

NEGLIGENCE. The failure to use such care as a reasonably prudent EMT would use under the same or similar circumstances.

OFF-LINE MEDICAL CONTROL. Control that involves general medical supervision of EMTs by a physician director who is experienced in prehospital care.

ON-LINE MEDICAL CONTROL. Control that involves direct and immediate EMT contact with a physician or nurse while the EMT is at the patient's side.

PARTY. The parties to a lawsuit include the plaintiff and defendant.

PLAINTIFF. In a civil lawsuit, the person bringing the suit.

PREHOSPITAL CARE SYSTEM DESIGN. The planned interrelationship between the various EMS system components, including pre-hospital care markets, levels and types of services, and dispatch and communications.

PREPONDERANCE OF THE EVIDENCE. Standard of proof in a civil lawsuit requiring the plaintiff to prove his or her case by the greater weight of the evidence or more likely than not.

PRIMA FACIE CASE. A plaintiff presents a prima facie case when he or she presents sufficient evidence to withstand a defendant's motion to dismiss the plaintiff's claims. In a negligence case, for example, sufficient proof to support a finding of duty, breach of duty, causation of injury and damages if contrary evidence is not presented or is disregarded. Once the plaintiff presents a prima facie case, the defendant is required to proceed.

PUNITIVE DAMAGES. In civil law, a form of damages designed to punish the defendant and to set an example for others.

QUALITY ASSURANCE. A program of checks and balances designed to assess patient care and improve its quality.

REFUSAL OF TREATMENT. The absence of consent to treatment.

SCOPE OF EMPLOYMENT. Employee actions in furtherance of duties owed to the employer under circumstances where the employer is or could be exercising some direct or indirect control over employee activities.

SCOPE OF PRACTICE. The outermost boundary of an EMT's authority that is set by state statutes and administrative rules.

SERVICE OF COMPLAINT. The formal process of delivering a complaint to a defendant in a civil lawsuit.

SETTLEMENT. An agreement reached between the parties to a dispute or a lawsuit finally disposing of the matter. In a negligence law-suit, for example, the plaintiff might agree to accept a certain sum of money to satisfy a damages claim against the defendant.

SPECIAL DAMAGES. A form of damages in negligence law, generally including lost wages, medical expenses, and property damage resulting from an EMT's breach of duty.

STANDARD OF CARE. Synonymous with an EMT's duty in negligence law. A violation of the standard of care means a breach of duty.

STATUTES OF LIMITATION. Statutory time limits placed on the right of an individual to bring a lawsuit. After the time limit passes, the prospective plaintiff loses the right to sue.

SUMMONS. A legal document that formally notifies a defendant of a lawsuit.

TORT CLAIMS ACTS. *See* GOVERNMENTAL IMMUNITY.

TRANSCRIPT. A typed word-for-word recording of everything said during a trial, hearing or deposition.

VICARIOUS LIABILITY. Indirect legal responsibility placed on one person for the acts of another person.

Index

About the Author

RICHARD A. LAZAR, J.D., is a practicing attorney in Portland, Oregon, whose national practice emphasizes emergency medical services (EMS) law and education. He is a member of the Oregon State Bar Association, the Oregon Trial Lawyers Association, and the Association of Trial Lawyers of America.

Mr. Lazar began working in prehospital care in 1972. He has worked as an emergency medical technician and as an emergency department trauma technician in both California and Oregon. Before beginning his law practice, Mr. Lazar was Director of Emergency Medical Services for the second largest county (Washington County) in Oregon.

Presently, Mr. Lazar is an instructor for two advanced paramedic training programs in the Portland metropolitan area where he teaches paramedic students EMS law. As Director of Med-Law, Inc., Mr. Lazar conducts EMS law seminars across the United States. Med-Law, Inc. provides medical/legal education programs to health care professionals throughout the country. He also participates as a speaker at EMS seminars and symposia nationwide.